How to Feed a

Dictator

Saddam Hussein, Idi Amin,

Enver Hoxha, Fidel Castro, and Pol Pot

Through the Eyes of Their Cooks

Witold Szabłowski

Translated by Antonia Lloyd-Jones

PENGUIN BOOKS

PENGUIN BOOKS
An imprint of Penguin Random House LLC
penguinrandomhouse.com

Originally published in Polish as *Jak nakarmić dyktatora*
by Grupa Wydawnicza Foksal, Warsaw

This publication has been supported by the © POLAND Translation Program.

ISBN 9780143129752 (paperback)
ISBN 9781101993392 (ebook)

Printed in the United States of America
3 5 7 9 10 8 6 4 2

Book design by Daniel Lagin

Menu

If "we are what we eat," cooks have not just made our meals, but have also made us. They have shaped our social networks, our technologies, arts and religions. Cooks deserve to have their story told often and well.

–**Michael Symons,**
A History of Cooks and Cooking

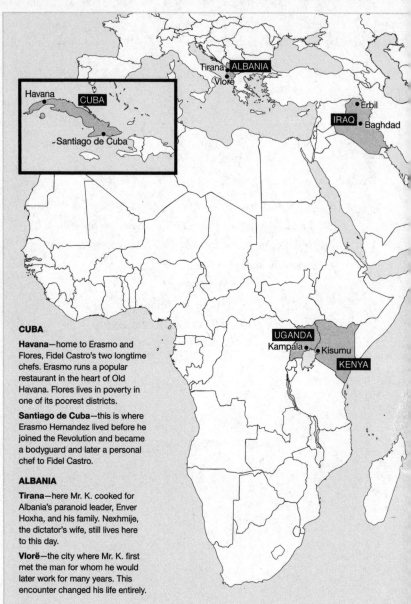

CUBA

Havana—home to Erasmo and Flores, Fidel Castro's two longtime chefs. Erasmo runs a popular restaurant in the heart of Old Havana. Flores lives in poverty in one of its poorest districts.

Santiago de Cuba—this is where Erasmo Hernandez lived before he joined the Revolution and became a bodyguard and later a personal chef to Fidel Castro.

ALBANIA

Tirana—here Mr. K. cooked for Albania's paranoid leader, Enver Hoxha, and his family. Nexhmije, the dictator's wife, still lives here to this day.

Vlorë—the city where Mr. K. first met the man for whom he would later work for many years. This encounter changed his life entirely.

Anlong Veng Ratanakiri Province

CAMBODIA • Phnom Penh

KENYA and UGANDA

Kisumu—Otonde Odera, the man who cooked for Ugandan presidents Milton Obote and Idi Amin, was born not far from this city. Many of the people employed in the Ugandan president's administration were from the Luo tribe, who inhabit the villages in this area. This is also where Barack Obama Sr., father of the forty-fourth US President, was from.

Kampala—the capital city of Idi Amin, the cruel dictator who threw his political enemies to the crocodiles and who to this day is suspected of cannibalism.

IRAQ

Baghdad—Abu Ali learned to cook here, before going on to work for Saddam Hussein. Abu Ali is the last of the Iraqi dictator's six personal chefs to remain alive.

Erbil—Abu Ali served in the army here during one of the Kurdish uprisings. He was assigned to the infantry but soon persuaded his commanders that he'd be more useful in the kitchen.

CAMBODIA

Anlong Veng—the last of the Khmer Rouge soldiers settled here. To this day this is home of Yong Moeun, Khmer Rouge leader Pol Pot's longtime cook and confidante.

Phnom Penh—the Cambodian capital, from where Pol Pot and his comrades ruled. During their regime, one quarter of the population lost their lives.

Ratanakiri Province—here, at an insurgent base, Auntie Moeun joined the Revolution and Brother Pol Pot, still known at the time by the pseudonym Pouk, meaning "Mattress." "He charmed me with his smile," says Moeun years on.

Starter

Knife and fork in hand? Napkin on your lap?

Ready or not, please be patient for just a while longer. First there's going to be a short introduction.

Before we move on to the main menu, I'll tell you the story of how I almost became a cook myself. In my early twenties, I had just graduated from university when I went to see some friends in Copenhagen. One thing led to another, and a few days later I found a job there washing the dishes at a Mexican restaurant in the city center. It was under the table, of course, but in four days I earned as much as my mom did in an entire month as a teacher in Poland. That helped me to tolerate the burned fat, the smell of which I could never wash out of my clothes or skin, and the crappy decor. At our restaurant you were constantly tripping over a cactus, and on the walls there were fake Colt holsters and sombreros on hooks, which at least one of the tequila-sodden customers would try to steal every single night. The way into the dining area was through saloon doors that were straight out of a Western; the kitchen was the only space with doors that could be closed.

And a good thing, too. Better for the clients not to know what went on in there.

There, over the cooking pots, cigarettes dangling from their lips, stood the chefs—all of them from Iraqi Kurdistan. They'd been drafted in by the owner, an Arab, who cruised about town in a swanky new BMW. He'd bought the place from an aging Canadian who'd grown tired of owning a Mexican restaurant in Copenhagen. I don't know how much he paid for it, but business was booming.

There were six chefs in total, and they all had their hands full from dawn to dusk. None of them had ever been to Mexico, and I suspect that if you'd handed them a map, they'd have had trouble pointing it out. I don't think any of them had ever been a chef before, either. But they were taught how to make burritos and fajitas, how to fry chicken Mexican-style, and how to add a small squirt of sauce to the tacos in a way that made it look as if they'd added lots. So they worked away, frying and squirting. The customers loved the food, and that was all that mattered. "There's no work in Iraq," the chefs would tell me, as if they had to explain themselves.

They taught me to smoke marijuana before starting work. "Otherwise it's unbearable," they'd say as they blew out smoke. They taught me to count to ten in Kurdish. They also taught me a few swear words, including the rudest one, which had something to do with your mother.

I spent the entire day working three dishwashing machines and scraping burned chicken out of the large pots by hand. In the rare spare moment, I tried to tame a rat that lived on the garbage heap by offering him scraps; I got this dumb idea from a movie. Luckily, the rat was smarter than I was and wisely kept his distance.

The Kurds were great co-workers; they planned my future career for me. "We'll teach you to cook," they promised. "You won't have to wash dishes all your life."

That's what I, too, was hoping. So I learned to make burritos, fry chicken, and squirt sauce on the tacos exactly as they did.

Until one day my cell phone rang. Someone had told the owner of another restaurant about the guy who was willing to work off the books. The other owner wanted to make me a better offer. This time I'd get as much as my teacher mom in Poland earned in a month in three days instead of four. Plus I'd be promoted to assistant cook. Without a second thought I said adios to the Kurds. Two days later I was putting on a black apron and taking up my post by the gas stove in a small but popular restaurant just off Nørrebrogade, one of the city's main arteries. This time there were two of us manning the kitchen: the owner, whose name was August, and me, Witold, his assistant.

August was half-Cuban and half-Polish, but he'd been raised in Chicago and didn't know a word of either Spanish or Polish. He'd spent most of his life working as a cook on cargo ships. The restaurant was meant to provide his pension.

Until the clients appeared, you could talk to August quite normally, but as soon as the lunch hour came—and out of our eight tables, let's say six were occupied—the devil got into him. The pans would rattle, the plates would fly, and August would scream. He'd hurl vulgar abuse at all his staff, with his wife bearing the brunt of it; she ran the bar and was also his business partner.

"August," I finally declared, after the latest of these outbursts, "if you speak to me that way once more, I'll fling my apron to the floor and be out of here."

August just smiled.

"Witold, I've worked in the kitchen all my life. I know who I can and cannot shout at." Seeing the amazed look on my face, he added, "We work together all day long, just the two of us, in forty square feet. I may yell at you, but you're the last person I want to pick a fight with."

So his fury was controlled! At that point it occurred to me that he could have been a diplomat just as well as a cook. It was the first time I'd seen how crafty and cunning chefs can be.

Once the situation in the dining room settled down, August's blood pressure would come down too. Then he'd tell stories about the sea; he'd spent half his life there, and he missed it. His tales were full of dolphins, whales, storms, and solitary yachtsmen whom he'd passed in his huge ship. There were tropical islands and frozen Greenland; the whole world was there. When we were free from customers, August became a wonderful, warm, intelligent guy with a great sense of humor. Then the diners would come back, and he'd go nuts again.

I observed his mood swings for several months. Every day we cooked together, and I helped him to come up with the dishes for a new menu. It was like magic: I felt as if we were painting the *Mona Lisa* together. One day August chilled a bottle of the strong stuff. We sat in the kitchen until late at night, while I chopped the vegetables and meat, and he used them to make ever more fanciful creations.

But there the comparison with painting ends. Leonardo didn't have to paint his *Mona Lisa* over and over again, seven days a week, but we churned out the dishes from August's menu dozens of times a day.

August taught me how to hold a knife without cutting myself and how to take bread out of the oven without burning myself. He taught me to cook steak and how to make salad and a great cream of leek soup. He even taught me what stance to adopt in the kitchen to make it easier to stay on my feet all day.

He also taught me that if there were any fancy fruits left on the plates after the Sunday brunch we were famous for—raspberries, for instance, or lychees, or Cape gooseberries in their papery brown cases—we should give them a rinse and put them on the next customer's plate.

"They're too expensive to throw out," he explained, seeing the horrified look on my face.

Until one day all eight of our tables were occupied in five minutes flat, and there was still a line of people standing in the doorway. August couldn't keep it in check.

"You fucking idler!" he yelled at me. Evidently, his fury was controlled to only a limited extent. "What are you gaping at? Go get the rolls!"

Too late—my apron was on the floor.

A few days later August called me and even said something that sounded quite like "sorry." Not that he had any special sympathy for me; I was just a low-cost worker, and it was in his financial interest to get me back.

But I hadn't the least desire to weather his mood swings again. I got a job driving tourists around Copenhagen in a rickshaw. Six months later I went back to Poland and became a journalist.

But I never forgot how fascinating cooks can be. They're poets, physicists, doctors, psychologists, and mathematicians all in one. Most of them have an unusual life story; it's a job where you have to give your all. Not everyone is suited to it, as my own example shows.

For many years as a news reporter, I wrote about social and

political issues. I never thought of working as a cook again, though I never stopped being interested in chefs. Then one day I saw a movie by the Slovak-Hungarian director Péter Kerekes called *Cooking History*. It was about army cooks, and it featured Branko Trbović, who was the personal cook of Marshal Josip Broz Tito, the absolute ruler of Yugoslavia.

He was the first dictator's chef I'd ever encountered. A lightbulb went on in my head.

I started wondering what the people who cooked at key moments in history might have to say. What was bubbling in the saucepans while the world's fortunes were in the balance? What did those cooks get a glimpse of as they were making sure the rice didn't dry out, the milk wasn't scalded, the chops didn't burn, or the water for the potatoes didn't boil over?

Other questions soon occurred to me. What did Saddam Hussein eat after giving the order for tens of thousands of Kurds to be gassed? Didn't he have a stomachache? And what was Pol Pot eating while almost two million Cambodians were dying of hunger? What did Fidel Castro dine on while sending the world to the brink of nuclear war? Which of them liked spicy food, and which preferred mild? Who ate a lot, and who just picked at his food? Who wanted his steak rare, and who liked it well done?

And finally, did the food they ate have any effect on their policies? Or did any of their cooks make use of the magic that comes from food to play a role in their country's history?

I had no choice. There were so many questions to be answered that I had to find the actual chefs who'd cooked for the dictators.

So off I went in search of them.

This book took almost four years to complete, in which time I crossed four continents, from a godforsaken village in the Kenyan savanna to the ruins of ancient Babylon to the Cambodian jungle where the last of the Khmer Rouge were in hiding. I shut myself away in the kitchens of the world's most unusual chefs. I cooked with them, drank rum with them, and played gin rummy with them. Together we went to the market and haggled over the price of meat and tomatoes. Together we baked fish and bread and made sweet-and-sour soup with added pineapple and goat-meat pilaf.

I had a hard time persuading each of them to talk to me. Some of them had never recovered from the trauma of working for someone who could have killed them at any moment. Some had served their regime loyally and to this day refuse to betray their secrets, even the culinary ones. And some simply didn't want to dredge up unpleasant memories.

I could write another entire book about how I persuaded them to open up to me. In the most extreme case, it took more than three years. But I managed it. I came to know twentieth-century history as it was seen from the kitchen. I learned how to survive in difficult times. How to feed a madman. How to mother him. And even how a well-timed fart can save the lives of more than a dozen people.

I found out where in the world dictators come from. At a time when, according to a report issued by the American organization Freedom House, forty-nine countries are ruled by dictators, this is vital information. What's more, the number keeps rising. Today's climate favors dictators, and it's worth knowing all we can about them.

So once again: Knife and fork at the ready? Napkin on your lap? All right, then.

Enjoy your meal.

Snack
អាហារសម្រន់

The first time I saw Brother Pol Pot, I was at a loss for words. I was sitting in his bamboo hut in the middle of the jungle, gazing at him. And I was thinking: what a beautiful man!

What a man!

I was very young then, so don't be surprised that's what I was thinking, brother. I was there to report to him on how people were feeling in the villages I'd passed through on my way to his base, and I was waiting for him to speak first. But he didn't say anything.

Finally, after a long time, he smiled gently at me. And at once I thought, what a beautiful smile he has!

What a smile!

I couldn't focus on what we were meant to be talking about. Pol Pot was very different from all the men I'd ever met before.

We met in the jungle, at a top secret base for Angkar, the organization we belonged to. In those days everyone still called Pol Pot Brother Pouk, which in Khmer means "mattress." For ages I wondered why he had such a strange nickname. I asked several people about it, but no one could tell me.

Many months later, one of the comrades explained to me that he was called Mattress because he always did his best to calm things down. He was soft. And that was his strength. When other people argued, he'd stand in the middle and help them to reach an agreement.

It's true. Even his smile was gentle; Pol Pot was pure goodness.

We had only a very short conversation that time. And when we were done, his adjutant took me to one side and said that Brother Pouk badly needed a cook. He'd had several, but none of them was right for him. So he asked if I'd like to give it a try.

"Yes," I said, "but I don't know how to cook."

"Surely you know how to make sweet-and-sour soup?" asked the adjutant, amazed, because it was the most popular soup in Cambodia.

"Give me a pot," I said.

And when he took me to the kitchen, I found that I knew perfectly well how to make that soup. You get some Chinese long beans, sweet potato, pumpkin, marrow, melon, pineapple, garlic, some meat—chicken or beef—and eggs. Two or three. You can add tomatoes, too, and lotus roots if you wish. First you boil the chicken, and then you add sugar, salt, and all the vegetables. I'm afraid I can't tell you how long you have to cook it for, because we didn't have watches in the jungle and I did everything by feel. I think it's about half an hour. To finish, you can add some tamarind root.

I also knew how to make papaya salad. You cut the papaya into very small pieces and then add cucumber, tomatoes, green beans, cabbage, morning glory, garlic, and a dash of lemon juice.

But the first time I made it, Pol Pot didn't eat it. Only later was it explained to me that he liked it prepared the Thai way: with dried crab or fish paste and peanuts.

I also knew how to make mango salad, how to bake fish, and how to roast chicken. Clearly as a child I'd watched how my mother did the cooking. Brother Pouk didn't expect any more than that. I was fit to be his cook.

I went into that kitchen and stayed there until nightfall. I made the lunch, then the supper; then I tidied up and washed the pots and pans.

And that's how I became Pol Pot's cook. I was very pleased that I could help. I wanted to stay at the base for the revolution. And for him, gentle Brother Mattress.

Breakfast

وجبة افطار

Thieves' Fish Soup

The Story of Abu Ali,
Saddam Hussein's Chef

One day, President Saddam Hussein invited some friends onto his boat. He took along several bodyguards, his secretary, and me, his personal chef, and we set off on a cruise down the river Tigris. It was warm—it was one of the first spring evenings that year. At the time we weren't at war with anyone, everyone was in a good mood, and Salim, one of the bodyguards, said to me, "Abu Ali, sit down, you've got the day off today. The president says he's going to cook for everyone. He's going to make *koftas* for us."

"A day off . . ." I smiled, because I knew that in Saddam's service there were no such words. And because there were going to be *koftas*, I started getting everything ready for the barbecue. I minced some beef and lamb and mixed them with tomato, onion, and parsley, then put it in the fridge so that it would stick to the skewers well later on. I prepared a bowl for washing one's hands, lit the fire, baked some pita bread, and made a tomato and cucumber salad. Only then did I sit down.

In Iraq every man thinks he knows how to barbecue meat. He's going to do it even if he doesn't know how. And it was the same with Saddam: people often ate the things he cooked out of politeness; after all, you're not going to tell the president you don't like the food he has made.

I didn't like it when he got down to cooking. But that time I thought to myself, "It's almost impossible to ruin *koftas*." If you have the meat ready, you squash it flat onto the skewer, press it with your fingers, then place it on the fire for a few minutes, and it's done.

The boat set off. Saddam and his friends opened a bottle of whiskey, and Salim came into the kitchen for the meat and salad.

I sat and waited to see what would happen next.

Half an hour later, Salim came back carrying a plate of *koftas*. "The president made some for you too," he said. I thanked him and said it was very good of the president, broke off a bit of meat, and wrapped it in pita bread. I tried it and . . . felt as if I'd burst into flames!

"Water, quick, water!"

I threw a glass of water down my throat, but it didn't help.

"More water!"

It was no good. I was still on fire. My cheeks and jaw were burning, and there were tears pouring from my eyes.

I was terrified. "Poison?" I thought. "But why? What for? Or maybe someone was trying to poison Saddam, and I've eaten it?"

"More water!"

Am I still alive?

"More water."

I am still alive . . . So it's not poison.

But in that case, what was he playing at?

It took me a good quarter of an hour to wash down the spicy flavor.

That was my first encounter with Tabasco sauce.

Saddam had been given it by someone as a gift, but because he didn't like very spicy food, he decided to play a joke by trying it out on his friends. And on his staff. Everyone on the entire boat was running around pouring water down their throat, while Saddam sat and laughed.

Twenty minutes later, Salim came back to ask if I'd liked the food. I was furious, so I said, "If I'd spoiled the meat like that, Saddam would have kicked me in the butt and told me to pay for it."

He did that sometimes. If he didn't like the food, he'd make you give back the money. For the meat, the rice, or the fish. "This food is inedible," he'd say. "You've got to pay fifty dinars."

So that's what I said, never expecting Salim to repeat it to the president. But when Saddam asked him how I'd reacted, Salim replied, "Abu Ali said that if he'd made something like that, you'd have kicked him in the butt and told him to pay for it." That's what he said, in front of all Saddam's guests.

Saddam sent Salim back again to fetch me.

I was scared. In fact, I was terrified. I had no idea how Saddam was going to react. You did not criticize him. Nobody did that: not the ministers, nor the generals, let alone a cook.

So off I went, terrified, annoyed with Salim for repeating what I'd said and annoyed with myself for mouthing off so stupidly. Saddam and his friends were sitting at the table, on which were the *koftas* and some open whiskey bottles. Some of the guests had red eyes; evidently, they'd eaten the Tabasco-flavored *koftas* too.

"I hear you didn't like my *koftas*," said Saddam in a very serious tone. His friends, the bodyguards, the secretary—everyone was looking at me.

I was getting more and more afraid. I couldn't suddenly start praising the food; they'd know I was lying.

I started thinking about my family. Where's my wife right now? What's she doing? Are the children home from school yet? I had no idea what might happen. But I wasn't expecting anything good.

"You didn't like them," Saddam said again.

And suddenly he started to laugh.

He laughed and laughed and laughed. Then all the people sitting at the table started laughing too.

Saddam took out fifty dinars, handed them to Salim, and said, "You're right, Abu Ali, it was too spicy. I'm giving back the money for the meat I wasted. I'll cook you some more *koftas*, but without the sauce this time. Would you like that?"

I said yes.

So he cooked me some *koftas* without any Tabasco. This time they were very good, but I tell you, it's impossible to ruin *koftas*.

1.

Wide streets, along which are hundreds of bombed-out houses that haven't been rebuilt and military checkpoints every few blocks. Canary-yellow cabs flash by, because here Baghdad insists that it's New York, and every cab must dazzle you with the color of ripe lemons.

After almost two years of searching, my guide and interpreter Hassan has found Saddam Hussein's last living cook for me. His name is Abu Ali, and for many years he refused to talk to anyone about the dictator, because he feared the vengeance of the Americans. It took Hassan a good twelve months to persuade him to talk.

Finally he agreed, but not without imposing conditions: we won't walk around the city, we won't cook together, and Hassan and I won't be able to visit him at home, though that's what I'd asked for. We'll just shut ourselves in my hotel room for the next few days; Abu Ali will tell me everything he remembers, and that will be the end of it.

"He's still afraid," explains Hassan. "But he's very keen to help," he quickly adds. "He's a good man."

So we're waiting for Abu Ali to arrive, and Hassan is boasting that he has escorted journalists from every country, on every front of every Iraqi conflict, from the American invasion to the civil war to the war against ISIS, and none of them has so much as broken a fingernail. To make sure I don't become the dishonorable exception, Hassan won't let me even cross the street on my own.

I don't believe him when he says the city is unsafe: right next to my hotel there's a Jaguar automobile showroom, and a little farther on, a large shopping mall. The place is swarming with policemen and armed security guards.

"I know everyone's smiling and friendly," says Hassan. "But don't forget that one percent of them are evil. Truly evil. To them, a solitary journalist from Europe is an easy target. You're going nowhere, I repeat, *nowhere* without me. Even together we're not going anywhere except in a licensed cab."

And he adds that only a few years ago foreigners here were kidnapped by the dozen. They were usually released as soon as the company that employed them paid a ransom. But not all of them came back.

And I am a freelancer. There won't be anyone to pay for me.

In spite of all that, you can't cheat nature. I'm simply not capable of sitting still, so as soon as Hassan goes home to his wife, I slip out for an evening stroll around the district where I'm staying. I pass a few mosques, some clothing stores, and people selling *mazgouf*, a local fish, which they bake on huge bonfires. I go into a nearby café for ice cream. I talk to a man selling sheep; he breeds them specially for the end of Ramadan, the holy month of fasting. I behave just as I would in any other country, on any other trip. Hassan shouldn't exaggerate, I think to myself.

Late that night I go back to the hotel and spend a long time writing up my impressions of my walk. I go to bed well after midnight.

Two hours later I'm woken by a tremendous bang. Soon after that I hear sirens. The lights and the Wi-Fi in my hotel are out.

Not until morning do I learn that a few hundred yards from my hotel a suicide bomber has killed more than thirty people.

2.

The next day Hassan is more than two hours late. Following the attack, police control has been tightened throughout the city, and as a result the traffic is frightful. Luckily, Abu Ali's late as well. We're waiting for him in the hotel lobby.

"This life is ghastly. You never know when and where the next bomb will go off," says my guide, sighing. "Since Saddam was deposed, everything's been plunged into chaos. Lots of the former army officers and secret policemen have joined paramilitary groups, and eventually ISIS. Now the Islamic State is weak, but only just over a year ago it looked likely to threaten Baghdad."

Many of the cities in Iraq are off-limits. I wanted to see Tikrit, for example, where Saddam was raised, but Hassan warns me that it's very dangerous.

"You have to have a guide who'll pay the hit squads that control the city," he says. "But even then there can be problems."

We're interrupted by Abu Ali's arrival. A jacket over a turtleneck. White hair, a small paunch, and an extremely amiable smile. We greet each other Iraqi-style: a handshake and a kiss on both cheeks. It flashes through my mind that for years, the hand I'm shaking fed one of the twentieth century's most notorious dictators. But we haven't the time to celebrate this moment. Abu Ali is uneasy. He doesn't want anyone to see him giving an interview or to ask who he is, for a foreigner to be recording a conversation with him. So we go and get a large jug of fresh orange juice, some water, an ashtray, and some snacks. Then we take the elevator to the third floor, and there we draw the curtains. I switch on the Dictaphone.

I was born in Hillah, not far from the ruins of ancient Babylon, but when I was a teenager, my parents moved to Baghdad, where my father opened a small grocery store, and one of his brothers, whose name was Abbas, opened a restaurant. The restaurant wasn't far from our house, so I used to go there almost every day. I liked the place, and when I was about fifteen or sixteen, I asked Abbas if he'd give me a job there.

Abbas put me in the kitchen. I learned to make the most typical Iraqi dishes, including shish kebab, kubbah, dolma, and *pacha*. Shish kebab is pieces of meat marinated in garlic and other seasonings, broiled on the fire, and served with rice or in a sandwich. Kubbah is meatballs made with tomatoes and bulgur wheat, served in a soup. Dolma is meat mixed with rice and wrapped in a vine leaf. *Pacha* is a delicacy—a soup made from a sheep's head, with its trotters and parts of its stomach added. You boil each of these items separately. You must cleanse them carefully, now and then skimming off the fat and the scraps that float to the surface. You use the skin of the stomach to make a little pocket, which you stuff with finely diced pieces of meat. You cook the *pacha* on a very slow flame, with hardly any seasoning, at most a little pepper, salt, lemon juice, and vinegar. Finally, you mix the three broths produced by boiling the head, trotters, and stomach, add the pocket stuffed with meat, and it's ready to serve. The greatest delicacy are the eyes.

My cooking was very successful. The customers liked me, and I liked my work. But after a few years I realized there was nothing more for me to learn at my uncle's restaurant, nor was I ever going to earn more there. I wanted to buy a car. So I decided to get a new job.

I read in a newspaper that the Baghdad Medical Center, the city's largest hospital, was looking for a chef. I applied. At the interview, they asked me only one question: Did I know how to cook rice for three hundred people?

Did I know how? I'd been doing it every day for the past eight years!

I was hired. I bought a car, but after a few years in the job that stopped being enough for me too. I started looking around for something different. I found a well-paid position at a five-star hotel and was just about to start when suddenly I was called up for the army.

I found myself in Erbil, a city in the north of Iraq, where the population are all Kurds. At the time they were staging an uprising, led by Mullah Mustafa, one of their top leaders.

Instead of starting a new job at a hotel, I went to war.

3.

The fighting against the Kurds took place mainly in the mountains. I was sent there with a rifle. I wasn't happy about it. I was twenty-six years old, I had nothing against the Kurds, and I certainly didn't want to get killed in a war against them.

So I told my commanding officer that in Baghdad I'd been a cook and that I was far better at cooking than shooting. They had thousands of soldiers but not many good cooks. The officer spoke to another officer, who spoke to someone else, until it turned out that Mohammed Marai, one of the commanders, had been complaining about the food. He didn't have a chef, and an adjutant was cooking for him.

Marai immediately ordered me to come and see him at the front. He had major problems with supplies: the peasants had abandoned their villages, and there was nowhere to get food.

So every day, while our men were fighting the Kurds, I got in a car and drove to Erbil—two hours each way—because that was the only place where you could buy anything. It was very dangerous. The Kurds could have fired at me at any moment.

Cooking something that tasted good on a field stove was close to impossible. I struggled for several weeks, until I timidly asked Marai if I could live in Erbil and cook normal meals there, in a normal kitchen, and bring them out to the front.

Marai agreed that it was a very good idea.

So I moved to Erbil, and every day a driver took me to the front and back. I'd pour Marai some soup, serve him salad, heat up the meat, and sit outside the tent—often with bullets flying past overhead. Was I afraid? No. You get used to the idea that you could die at any moment. You focus on where to get a chicken or a fish for the next meal, rather than on death.

Until one day my military service was over. I said goodbye to Marai and the rest, and then I was taken in an army car to Mosul. From there I caught a train back to Baghdad. Just like that. You board a train, and you come home from the war. It was extraordinary, and many years later, when I was already working for Saddam, I was still amazed that we could get into a car in safe Baghdad and a few hours later be in a war zone, where people were being killed.

Unfortunately, there was no job at the hotel waiting for me. But one of Marai's adjutants suggested to me that if I wanted to work at a hotel, I should apply to the Ministry of Tourism. "They employ cooks for all the government hotels throughout the country," he said, and gave the name of a friend of his who'd be able to help me.

And that was how, only two months after the war, I ended up at one of the government palaces—the Palace of Peace— taking a special course for chefs.

4.

Navarin is a dish of lamb with cherry tomatoes and potatoes boiled in broth. It's delicious. I can still remember the day when one of the teachers showed us how it's made. It was a great discovery—that you can cook lamb, our national meat, in a different way, not just by the only method I had known about before.

There were two teachers, John from England and Salah from Lebanon. John taught us about meat and European cuisine, and Salah taught us to make desserts and Arab cuisine. We learned how to make chicken roulade, chocolate mousse, sponge cake, and quiche.

I completed the course with the highest grade of all the students. Instead of sending me to a hotel, which was my dream, the teachers said it would be better for me to stay at the school and teach introductory classes for the next group of students. I also worked as a cook for the Ministry of Tourism.

I ended up on a team that included the best cooks in Iraq. We worked for all the official delegations: government ministers, parliament leaders, presidents, and kings. The king of Jordan came on an official visit, and soon after the king of Morocco came too. I was very excited, because until then I'd only cooked at the hospital, at the front, and at my uncle Abbas's restaurant. I could hardly have expected to progress from working at those places to cooking for kings!

But often I had no idea whom I was cooking for. Being a cook is a bit like being in the army: better not think too much; just carry out the orders.

Until one day my colleague, whose name was Nisa, and I were given an unusual task: our bosses told us to make the finest cake we possibly could. We worked on it for two days and two nights. We joined sponge cakes with cream to make a square, each side of which was six feet long. Then we made a vertical structure, nine feet high. And onto this frame we built ancient Mesopotamia. We carved the old ruins out of sponge cake and made rivers out of marzipan, as well as trees, palms, and animals out of fruit. We decorated the top with an almond flower, and right at the center we made a waterfall out of coconut shavings.

Two days later we saw our cake on television.

And there, cutting it himself, was President Saddam Hussein. It was his birthday cake.

5.

While we're waiting for our next meeting with Abu Ali, Hassan kills time by telling me about aliens.

"You can laugh, I'm used to people not believing me. But they really do exist. And they really are interested in us. They fly here to watch us. I am one of very few people who can see them. At every battlefield I've been to, I've seen them standing off to one side, watching what we're doing."

"Are they friendly?" I ask skeptically, because I have to ask something.

"Yes. They know I can see them. They saved my life several times. They feel for us. They don't want us to get killed or to kill each other."

It crosses my mind that someone could write a great story about this man who has seen so much evil that in order to get his head around it, he has started seeing aliens. But I'm soon reproaching myself: maybe he really does see them, and it's just me, with my stupid rationality, who refuses to believe him. From now on I agree with Hassan, whatever he says.

But I'm not here to learn about aliens. So I say, "Tell me about Saddam."

"He was a real son of a bitch," he says, shaking his head. "He was born near Tikrit, and that has always been a city of thieves and smugglers. They've always been proud that the great Arab leader Saladin was born in their city too. Saddam was raised to worship him, and he probably had too much faith in the idea that he was the next leader of the Islamic world. Maybe that's why he ended up as he did: whatever was going on, he believed that Allah was guiding him. But even so, his career was incredible. His father abandoned his mother when she was pregnant. In an Iraqi village, where to this day medieval rules apply, that must have been very hard for them."

Saddam Hussein's biographers would agree with Hassan: from the start of his life Saddam had to be the strongest. After her divorce from his father, his mother, Sabha, formed a relationship with a man known as the Liar; apparently, he tried to convince people that he'd been on the pilgrimage to Mecca, though everyone knew it wasn't true. The Liar wasn't rich—he had one donkey and two or three sheep—so he thought up a plan for his wife's son to help him increase his property. Instead of sending the boy to school, he taught him to steal. "There are stories of him stealing chickens and eggs to feed his family, others of him selling watermelon on the train which stopped in Tikrit on its way from Mosul to Baghdad."*

On top of that, the Liar was always humiliating the boy, forcing him to dance and hitting him for no reason.

Saddam would have ended up as a petty thief if not for his uncle Khairallah Talfah. This well-read, politically minded man from Tikrit took Saddam to live with him, despite having a small flock of children of his own. At his uncle's house Saddam learned that there was another world beyond the Iraqi village. And although his new

---

* Saïd K. Aburish, *Saddam Hussein: The Politics of Revenge* (Bloomsbury, 2001), 17.

guardian's horizons were not particularly broad either—he sympathized with the Nazis and even wrote a pamphlet titled *Three Whom
God Should Not Have Created: Persians, Jews, and Flies*—it was his
influence that awakened Saddam's curiosity about the world.

A few years later, when his uncle was arrested for taking part in
an antigovernment plot, Saddam had to return to his mother and
stepfather. But he had come to regard Khairallah's children, especially his son Adnan, as his best friends. His uncle had shown him
what it meant to have a family.

Saddam would be grateful to him for a long time to come.

6.

It all began quite innocently.

One of the waiters, whose name was Shah Juhani, told me
I was to report to a palace on the outskirts of the city, near the
airport. He said they had extra work for me there.

I didn't give it any special thought, because now and
then I had an extra commission at the ministry. Sometimes
a foreign minister arrived, sometimes an entire delegation,
and sometimes we had to make candy for someone's birthday. So I went along without thinking what they'd require
of me this time. Someone let me in through the gate, and
someone else checked that I wasn't carrying a weapon. On
the spot I was greeted by a man named Kamel Hana. He
shook my hand and said, "Abu Ali, you need to know that I
work in President Saddam Hussein's security. I'm taking you
to see him."

"Sorry?" I said. I thought it was a joke.

"I'm taking you to see President Saddam Hussein," he repeated, very solemnly. "Everything that happens and everything the president says is confidential."

I couldn't believe my ears. I'd been working at the ministry for several years, but I'd never met anyone who cooked for the president. How had I suddenly got here?

I had to sign a special confidentiality agreement forbidding me to tell anyone anything about what I would see in Saddam's house. It said that if I broke this promise, I would incur the penalty of death by hanging.

It all happened at the speed of lightning. Less than ten minutes after I had entered the palace, I was standing in front of Saddam.

Only later did I put the pieces together. About six months earlier, my bosses had asked me to write up a résumé, listing all the people I had ever worked with and the names of my family members. I also had to bring in a certificate from the police stating that I had never been convicted of anything. The police had been to see my father and Abbas and had asked questions about me—what I'm like, whether I can drink without causing trouble or getting into a fight, whether I'd had contact with foreigners, Kurds, or religious radicals or been in trouble with the law. And finally, whether any customers had ever complained that I'd poisoned them. The police had also been to the hospital and talked to my friends.

At the time I thought it was normal procedure; because I was cooking for kings, they had to ask about that sort of thing, in case it turned out I was crazy.

But they were already grooming me to be the president's chef. It had all been carefully prepared many months in advance—except that I'd had no idea about it. Saddam liked things to happen by surprise. Then he had the advantage.

But I didn't know that yet. That day I suddenly found myself standing before the president.

"So you're Abu Ali?" he said.

"Yes, Mr. President," I stammered.

"Excellent. Make me a tikka."

I bowed and went to the kitchen.

7.

Kamel Hana came to the kitchen with me. It turned out that his father had been Saddam's chef too; although he was still working, he was about to retire, and I was to replace him. That was to happen a few months from now, but the president's other cook was sick, and because Hana had already vetted me thoroughly, he'd decided to fast-track my appointment.

He accompanied me the whole time and told me about the place and about working for Saddam, while I made tikka: you chop the meat into very small pieces, add salt and pepper, skewer it as for small kebabs, and cook it over an open flame. I made a tomato and cucumber salad to go with it. Half an hour later it was all ready, and Kamel took it to Saddam. Twenty minutes after that he came back. "The president wants to see you," he said.

A cook always feels awkward talking to someone who has just eaten his cooking. And imagine how he feels if that person is the president of the country!

But Saddam was pleased.

"Thank you, Abu Ali. You really are a very good cook," he

said, though tikka isn't a complicated dish. And he gave me an envelope with fifty dinars inside. Nowadays that would be almost $150.

"I hope you'll agree to come and work for me?" he asked.

And I bowed and, without hesitation, said, "Of course, Mr. President."

Could I have refused Saddam? I don't know, but I preferred not to try.

8.

That was how, instead of going to work at the hotel of my dreams, I ended up in the president's kitchen.

We called the place where Saddam lived "the farm." A residence was being constructed there, but it was before the time when he had all those huge palaces. It had very large grounds, which did include a real farm, where some people from Tikrit raised hens, goats, sheep, and cows. Zijad the butcher and his four assistants slaughtered a lamb and several chickens each day so we could have fresh meat. There were date palms, a small vegetable garden, and a little lake where we could catch fish when Saddam felt like eating *mazgouf*—grilled fish, which he loved.

It was a very nice place.

There were six cooks—the smallest team I had ever worked on. What's more, two of the cooks spent the whole time working for Saddam's wife, Sajida, who was also his cousin—the daughter of his uncle Khairallah Talfah. One of those cooks was named Shakir, and he had been the head cook for the previous president, al-Bakr. Saddam hadn't fired him but probably didn't fully trust him, so he and a second cook, Habib, worked for the First Lady. I saw them only once every few weeks.

Sajida had her own residence. She suspected her husband of having affairs, but because he was working all the time, he was hardly ever at home, so she knew nothing for sure. Anyway, she was annoyed with him all the time. Whenever she could, she traveled about the world on major shopping trips.

The four other cooks, including me, worked on two shifts, one day on and the next day off. The cook who worked with me was Marcus Isa, a Christian from Kurdistan. And Kamel Hana liked me very much and often came to see us. From them I learned that the fifty-dinar tip I'd been given the first time I made tikka for Saddam was no fluke. They told me that if he was in a good mood, Saddam wanted others to be happy too, and then he'd hand out money left and right. If you make something he likes on one of those days, you'll get a reward, they said.

Marcus and I divided the tips fairly, fifty-fifty. If I got extra money, I gave half of it to my co-worker, and he did the same for me.

So a large part of working for Saddam involved sensing if he was having a good day, and then we'd cook something he particularly liked. And on the other days we'd keep out of his way. No, I wasn't afraid he'd harm me. But on a bad day, if he didn't like the taste of something, he might insist that I give back the money for the meat or the fish to the administration bursary. It happened often. He'd eat something, decide it was too salty, and summon me to his presence.

"Abu Ali, who the hell adds that much salt to tikka?" he'd ask. Or to an omelet, or okra soup, which was one of his favorites. It didn't matter what the dish was; he'd ask that question about the salt, but without giving me a chance to reply, he'd snap, "You'll repay me for it. Kamel, make sure he pays fifty dinars."

He was usually wrong; he just made a fuss when he was having a bad day. But I had to pay. Marcus and I even made jokes about it. Whenever the phone in the kitchen rang and we were told one of us must go and see the president, before picking it up, Marcus would shout, "Fifty dinaaaars!"

But a few days later Saddam would be in a better mood, and remembering that he'd docked money from my salary, he'd say to Kamel Hana, "Our Abu Ali made a wonderful lentil soup today. He added just the right amount of salt. Give him back the money you took from him the other day, and throw in another fifty dinars."

Those soups were probably identical, but that's what Saddam was like. You never knew what to expect from him. One day he'd take; the next day he'd give. At the end of the month I was always ahead of the game, getting more than my salary.

Twice a year we were given a set of new clothes made specially for us in Italy. We were also given clothes for the kitchen—aprons, hats, and caps—and two suits with vests. Saddam sometimes took us abroad with him, so we had to look good. Once a year a tailor from Italy came to the palace and measured everyone who worked for Saddam, then made clothes for us all at his workshop and sent them by air.

And once a year—you'll envy me—once a year Saddam bought each of us a new car. Each year a different one: among others I had a Mitsubishi, a Volvo, and a Chevrolet Celebrity. On that day the administration took away the keys to our old cars and gave us the keys to the new ones. Nobody asked you

about it; you just came to work, and when you left, there was
a new car parked in the garage.

9.

To understand Saddam better, I'm meeting with Hassan Yasin, a
doctor from Iraq who lives in Istanbul. We're sitting in one of the
cafés on Istanbul's famous İstiklal Avenue, and Yasin is showing
me a picture of himself as a seven-year-old, handing Saddam a
bunch of flowers.

"He visited my school," he says. "My mom was the deputy head.
It was a great honor; I couldn't sleep for a whole week. At the time
I didn't know much about him yet; to me he was the man from the
TV and the banknotes."

A few years later Yasin's mom fell into disfavor with Saddam's
regime for criticizing the war against Kuwait in a private conversation. A distant relative, who was an officer in the security services,
warned her that she was going to be arrested, so she took her two
sons and some essential items and left for Turkey in a hurry. They
escaped without telling her husband, who was a member of the
Ba'ath Party and a great admirer of Saddam's.

"I never saw my father again," says Yasin. "They suspected him
of having known about our escape in advance. Apparently, he
started to drink heavily. He died a few months later, officially in a
car crash, but I think he was killed by the Iraqi secret services."

"And why do you think Saddam rose so high?"

Yasin has a ready answer to that.

"He was ruthless. He modeled himself on Stalin; he liked to read
biographies of him. He thought like a chess player, several moves

ahead. From the moment he entered politics, he never took a single step backward."

Saddam was also famous for his cruelty. The Ba'ath Party made him head of its security apparatus. He was in charge of the torture of its political opponents and of purges within the party. He used to beat the prisoners with a rubber hose filled with stones. Or stick a glass bottle in their anus and smash it by kicking them.

"My father always spoke of Saddam's services with the greatest respect," says Yasin.

The secret police that the dictator founded was named Jihaz al-Haneen, "Instrument of Yearning." All its members were recruited from the al-Tikritis, Saddam's clan.

"That was how he guaranteed himself loyalty," explains Yasin. "In Iraq your clan is sacred. Saddam was in charge of torture, but meanwhile he was very quietly building his position within the party. That was something else he'd learned from Stalin, who knew how to concentrate a vast amount of power in his own hands without flaunting it. People were surprised when, after Lenin's death, Stalin turned out to be stronger than Trotsky. Saddam adopted a similar tactic. By the time people realized how much influence he had, it was too late to bar his way."

In 1968, the Ba'ath Party took power for the second time in its history. A distant cousin of Saddam's, Ahmad Hasan al-Bakr, became president. And at only thirty-one years old, Saddam became vice president of Iraq. He was responsible for the purges: In 1969, dozens of Iraqi Jews were executed. That same year the army brutally crushed the Kurds.

From 1970 to 1972, Saddam fought against the Shi'ites.

In 1974, the purges included communists and other—more or less legitimate—enemies of the Ba'ath Party.

Saddam didn't just kill and torture. He also took to heart the idea that "full bellies don't foment revolution" and considered how to fill the Iraqis' bellies well enough for them not to want to overthrow the Ba'ath Party. He decided to nationalize Iraq's entire crude oil industry. From then on, the money derived from oil extraction would go not to Western companies, as in the past, but into the pockets of every Iraqi.

"The diabetic president Ahmad Hasan al-Bakr was no more than a figurehead by then," says Yasin.

In 1977, Saddam replaced the top army commanders with his own supporters.

Two years later he took full control.

10.

When I started the job, Iraq was at war with Iran. We were often at the front. Saddam went there in an ordinary military vehicle, but if he wanted to stay the night somewhere near the front, he slept in a camper van. There was no question of any great luxury.

Those trips reminded me of my days in the army. I'd arrive at work in the morning, and someone—usually Kamel Hana—would say, "Pack up. We're going to the war." So I'd pack. If there was an hour or more before departure, I'd prepare some of the food so I'd have less to do on-site. Out there we cooked on a field stove, and that's much harder. I always did my best to have at least the rice ready in advance.

We'd drive there and Saddam would go visit the soldiers. I'd remain at a slight distance, set up the stove, and finish the cooking I'd started earlier. Or I'd light a bonfire to cook tikka, or *koftas*, or fish.

The president wanted to show that he cared about his soldiers so much that he cooked rice for them in person. We'd have a pot of rice that I had parboiled earlier. We'd set up the stove, and Saddam would finish off cooking the rice and then pour on the sauce, also prepared by me. But Saddam would always start chatting to an officer or posing for pictures—he loved being photographed—and he often burned the rice. Or he'd talk nonstop while sprinkling a whole kilo of salt into the pot. And then he'd serve the burned or oversalted rice to the soldiers. They had to eat it; after all, the president had cooked it for them.

We had a special pot for those outings: a large one with a very thick bottom so the rice wouldn't burn. Even so, every few trips we had to replace it.

If Saddam was going straight to the front, they'd drop me off a mile or two away, and I'd cook there. Once I had everything ready, I drove the food to the front, just like when I was in the army.

It could be dangerous. One time Saddam was visiting a unit that had won a skirmish about fifteen hours earlier. Suddenly, out of the blue, the Iranians counterattacked. Khomeini had convinced them that anyone who was killed in the war would go straight to heaven, even if he hadn't been religious in the past, even if he hadn't observed the rules of Islam at all. So they attacked with extreme fury, because they were angry with Iraq, and they believed that if they were killed in battle, they'd wake up in heaven. They screamed and ran at us pell-mell.

Everyone panicked. Some of the soldiers started firing, but some—including me, to my shame—ran for their lives. I threw away my cooking pot and ran off. I was sure they were going to kill us on the spot.

All sorts of things are said about Saddam these days. For instance, they say he was lily-livered and never fought in any war as a soldier himself, but just sent others out to war.

But I saw Saddam in a situation where everyone else fled. Including me.

He stayed put.

Once the danger had passed, I went back with my head down. Saddam was standing in the same place where I had last seen him, discussing the situation with the soldiers. He didn't even glance at me or at the other soldiers who had run away. I heard that some of them were later executed. I don't know if that's true. I had no problems. I set up the cooking pot again; the fire was still smoldering, but the rice was on the ground. I had to start cooking all over again.

I told Marcus what had happened, and he said, "You did very well, Abu Ali. You're not there to save the president. He has bodyguards for that. Our task is to do the cooking. If you'd tried doing something else, you might have done it badly."

He was right.

11.

Almost as soon as I started working for the president, I met his wife, Sajida. As I've already said, they were permanently at odds, and on the whole Sajida avoided him. But Saddam wanted me to learn to make his favorite soup—fish soup from

Tikrit—and Sajida knew exactly how to make it the way they'd had it in childhood, at her family home.

So she came to the farm and told me what ingredients to prepare; then she came to the kitchen, and we stood over the pots together.

It's an unusual soup, familiar only to people from Tikrit; I've never tasted anything like it, before or since. Saddam called it "thieves' fish soup," because apparently Tikrit's local thieves used to make it. We use the oiliest fish, gattan, for this soup. But I know you can make it with other fish, salmon or cod. First you cut it into inch-long pieces; then you coat it in flour. You put some onion and a dash of oil at the bottom of the pot. You fry the onion, then place a layer of fish on top. You sprinkle it with parsley. Then you add a layer of tomatoes. Then a layer of dried apricots. Then tomatoes again. Then fish again. Then a layer of almonds. Then fish again.

As you arrange the layers, it's important for the onion to remain at the bottom. And for the soup to include garlic, parsley, almonds, apricots, and tomatoes. You can also add a few raisins.

Then you wait until the water from the fish and vegetables you've added has evaporated. When you hear a hissing sound, which means there's no water left, you pour hot water from the kettle over it all, until you've covered the top layer.

After pouring in the water, you cook it for another fifteen to twenty minutes. Finally, you can add a little turmeric.

That's the soup Sajida taught me to make.

Nowadays, apart from her, I'm the only person on earth who knows how to make it the way Saddam Hussein liked it.

You're the third.

12.

All the president's top bodyguards and officials were from Tikrit. Even the people who did the shopping for the palaces, even the members of the dance troupe that he sometimes took with him when he went on a tour of Iraqi cities. They were all from Tikrit, and most of them were closely or distantly related to Saddam.

Apart from the al-Tikritis, as they were called, Saddam trusted Christians too. Except for me, all the kitchen staff were Christians, mostly from the north of Iraq, from Kurdistan. I was the only Muslim, and I didn't have a connection to Tikrit. Perhaps I really am a pretty good cook, because I can't find another reason for them to have employed me there.

Those al-Tikritis were not good people. I remember his bodyguards: Habib, Saad, Naser, Abdullah, Rafat, Ahmed, Isma, Haji, Akram, and Salim. I remember his secretary, Abd Ahmud. You wouldn't want to meet any of them on a dark night.

The bodyguards had their own kitchen, which we called "14," because that was the number you called to reach their cooks, but sometimes they asked us to cook something for them.

I had to refuse. The president's cook was the president's cook; I was to cook for the head of state, his family, and guests only, and not for the bodyguards or anyone else on the staff. Just as you don't wear the president's shorts or shoes, and you don't drive his car, you don't eat his food made by his cook. Those were the rules, though sometimes, when they saw that I was making something good, they tried to persuade me to give them some. They wouldn't tell anyone, and we should support each other, they said.

But I always stuck to my guns. Rules are rules.

Then they'd get angry, start swearing, and I could see they weren't the sort of people you could make friends with or whom you could trust.

Saddam's sons, Uday and Qusay, were horrible too, especially Uday. Once he was driving his car through the city when he spotted an attractive girl who was walking hand in hand with a soldier. He stopped the car and kidnapped her, while his bodyguards took away the soldier. Uday had his way with the girl, and soon after she committed suicide. Her fiancé was shot.

Uday could kill with his bare hands. If any of his staff did something he didn't like, Uday would beat them up himself—usually with a metal stair rod. It happened to one of his cooks, for instance, a man I knew; Uday didn't like the food he'd made, so he beat him unconscious.

Both Uday and Qusay often spent time at our palace. Whenever I ran into Uday, he'd look at me in a way that told me that if his father weren't protecting us, he'd kill us all.

The only good person in the entire al-Tikriti family was Saddam. I don't know how he survived among them.

13.

Abu Ali is busy for the next few days, so I gather my courage and set off to see southern Iraq. Saif accompanies me as my guide. He's from the Basra area, twenty years old, with a trendy beard and an even trendier haircut; he makes his living as a tattoo artist and is a real Baghdadi hipster, though—like any hipster—if you ask him about it, he strenuously denies it.

"Of course the occasional bomb goes off in Baghdad," he tells me, "but the south is safe. Nothing'll happen to us there. I had a girlfriend in Basra and I used to go and see her twice a week."

Even the ever-cautious Hassan says we ought to be safe in the south.

So we're off.

A yellow share taxi takes us from Baghdad to Hillah, the city where Abu Ali the cook was born and where you can see the ruins of ancient Babylon. The driver is wearing a gray sweater and a black fake leather jacket. It's winter; the temperature in Iraq has fallen below sixty degrees Fahrenheit and everyone's freezing.

"What's his occupation?" the driver asks Saif while also spitting the remains of some sunflower seeds out of the window.

Saif explains that I'm doing an interview with Saddam Hussein's cook and I want to see what Iraq looks like since he was deposed and since the war.

"Tell him I'm waiting for a new Saddam to come." He spits out of the window again. "I hope I live to see the day," he adds, and two other passengers nod with approval.

"Why is that?" I ask.

"If he were alive, there wouldn't be any Scheissis-Aysis." He must mean ISIS, the so-called Islamic State, whose territory, at the time of our conversation, starts about 125 miles away. "In Saddam's day every rascal went straight to jail. There wasn't such a shambles as there is now. When he was alive, everyone said he was sending us to war while he built palaces. I was in the war against Iran too. I was only eighteen. I got shot in the hand."

And he shows us the scars: where the bullet went in and where it came out. To give us a closer look, he briefly lets go of the steering wheel, which at eighty miles an hour seems rather risky. Luckily, he soon grabs it with the other hand.

I'm trying to protest. I know from the history books and the press that Saddam was a brutal dictator who killed and tortured the Iraqis. But the driver waves dismissively and spits out of the window again, as if to say that talking to me is pointless.

The two remaining passengers, both over sixty, come to my aid.

"When I was young and Saddam was running the country, half the girls in Baghdad went about in miniskirts," says one, who introduces himself as a power engineer. "We lived like in Europe. But nowadays half of them go about in Islamic dress that hides the whole body. Not a single one goes out in a miniskirt anymore. It's an awful pity. If I want to look at women's legs, I have to find them on the internet." He smirks under his mustache, probably at the thought of what he sees there.

"We're being ruled by mullahs," says the other, an engineer who specializes in building bridges.

"We fought in the war against Iran, and now Shi'ites from Iran are taking away our government." The driver has stopped staring out the window and returns to the conversation. "That's all the U.S. achieved with its war. Iraq is now being run by Iran, America's enemy."

Once again I try to protest, but unexpectedly Saif, my Baghdadi hipster, speaks up.

"Fuck all you know!" he says to me heatedly. "My father was an officer in Saddam's day. And of course, if anyone got on his bad side, or upset one of his sons, they came to a nasty end. But a country like Iraq can only be ruled with an iron fist. Otherwise it's a total fuckup. Like now."

I think even the engineers and the driver are surprised to hear this from the twenty-year-old, who has no cause to remember Saddam or to have any love for him. For the rest of the journey we're silent; the engineers doze off. Only the driver, between efforts to spit out sunflower seeds, asks Saif, "So what does your father do now?"

"He's a cabdriver like you."

"Give him my best regards."

14.

For breakfast he usually had eggs, fish, or soup—lentil or okra.

For lunch we always made six, seven, or eight different dishes. There were two soups, two kinds of chicken, some fish, and something from the barbecue. He always had a choice.

At least once a week there was *mazgouf,* grilled fish, for supper. He loved it. If he didn't get it for several days, he would tell Kamel Hana or his chief bodyguard to ask us when we were going to make it.

Saddam looked in at the kitchen only during Ramadan, when he was fasting from sunrise to sunset. He'd drop in when he was very hungry and wanted to improve his mood. But those visits were the exception.

Before we served Saddam his food, Kamel Hana tested it. If he wasn't there, one of us cooks was ordered to eat some. Apparently, gifts that came from abroad, such as wine, whiskey, or Cuban cigars, which Saddam adored, were also tested for poison. His security guards took them to a laboratory, but I don't know the details.

The shopping for the kitchen was done exclusively by Saddam's bodyguards, and only the most trusted ones. If something wasn't available on the farm, they'd go to the market or to a tried-and-true place. But where and how the shopping was done were things we cooks didn't know.

We always had to leave samples of food in the fridge—just in case.

Saddam was amazingly healthy. In my time at the farm, he felt unwell only once. It was such an unusual event that just in case we were all arrested that night, and the secret police checked that none of us had poison on his hands.

Every year we went to Tikrit or somewhere outside Baghdad, where he swam across the Tigris River, which is very wide and has a strong current.

One year, following the invasion of Kuwait, the Americans had been spreading rumors that it wasn't Saddam who swam the Tigris but his double. They said Saddam was too old to swim across the river. And do you know what he did? A few weeks later, he invited the journalists and diplomats to the outskirts of Tikrit. He showed himself to them and made a speech so that everyone could see that it was definitely him. Then he entered the water and swam across the river, in both directions.

And you know what? They started to say there was a hidden platform in the middle of the river with an engine that had pulled him along. So you see, it's impossible to convince people that a man can simply be in good health if he's strong and exercises every day. Saddam had a swimming pool at each of his palaces. He went for a swim before breakfast. Every single day.

I cooked for him, I saw him every other day for years on end, and only once did I ever hear of him being sick. In a bad mood—yes, many times. But sick—hardly ever.

15.

I went to many countries with Saddam, including Morocco, Jordan, and the Soviet Union. In Moscow we were hosted by Gorbachev. They talked about weapons, because the war against Iran was under way.

In the Soviet Union even the cooks behaved like the cooks for a superpower. We all cooked on one large gas stove, and now and then they moved our pots. There was no need to do that; there was plenty of room for everyone. But that's what they were like. Their country was pushy in politics, and they were pushy in the kitchen. They moved their own pots to take up the space—and the fire—set aside for ours.

Of course as soon as they moved one of my pots, I went up and moved it back again. A few minutes would go by, and then one of the Russian cooks would go up and move their pots onto our burners again, muttering something as he did it. He was probably cursing us—I don't know, I can't understand Russian.

That game went on for hours.

At the time it occurred to me that that's just how wars erupt: each side wants his pots closer to the fire.

16.

One of the reasons why Saddam liked Kamel Hana was that Hana brought him women. After all, the president couldn't just go up to a stranger and tell her he was interested in her. Kamel knew the president's taste, and he also knew a lot of people in Baghdad, and sometimes he'd bring a lady to the farm so the president could talk to her in a more relaxed atmosphere.

To do what? I'm sorry, I'm telling you too much anyway.

One day Kamel introduced Saddam to a woman named Samira Shahbandar. She was married, but that was no obstacle for Saddam, or for her either.

They were very attracted to each other. Samira started visiting the farm almost every day. Wherever he went, Saddam took her with him. All this took place in secret from his first wife, Sajida. Even a few months later, when Saddam arranged for Samira to divorce her first husband, and even when he then married her, Sajida didn't know about it. Sajida was the daughter of his uncle, to whom he owed so much. Her brother, Adnan, was the minister of defense, a hero of the war against Iran. Saddam didn't want to spoil his relationship with any of them.

Samira was from a distinguished Baghdadi family that had come to Iraq from Persia—in other words, Iran—several decades earlier. In the meantime they had lost almost all their wealth, and as a little girl Samira had lived in poverty. It was only thanks to her parents' devotion that she'd been able to finish school and then go to college. When she began to earn a good living as a doctor, she bought her parents food, household equipment, and even clothes.

Later she became the president's wife, but she went on behaving like a girl from a poor home. Sometimes she came to see us in the evening and asked what we had left to eat, and when we showed her, she'd pack it all in containers and send a driver to take it to her parents.

By doing this, she drove Saddam mad. He treated her family very well. He bought her parents a new house, and once a year he gave her brothers and sisters new cars, just as he did for us. He made sure they had everything they needed; Samira's three children from her first marriage came to live with us at the farm, and Saddam paid for their schooling and college.

And what's more, when her ex-husband fell sick, Saddam told us to cook for him, and one of the drivers took him food each day. Can you imagine?

Samira had no reason to take food from the farm and deliver it to her parents. She was simply so accustomed to being poor that she didn't know how else to behave. Saddam used to get terribly upset with her. "Act like the president's wife!" he'd scream. "If there's anything your family needs, tell me, and I'll buy it for them!"

Samira would cry, and he'd go on shouting.

After a quarrel of that kind, Samira wouldn't come to see us for several days or weeks. But her compulsion must have been stronger than she was, because she'd wait for Saddam to go away and then come to the kitchen again and ask what food we had left. And once again she'd pack it all in containers and tell the driver to take them to her parents.

17.

With Saif, the Baghdadi hipster, I go on a tour of Hillah, or rather the ruins of ancient Babylon that adjoin the city. We take a souvenir selfie at the spot where—apparently—Alexander the Great died. We also take pictures of the remains of the Ishtar Gate and the incredible figures of the gods that guarded it. Although it's one of the places where our civilization was born, for years Babylon has been trying in vain to be added to UNESCO's list of world heritage sites. All because of Saddam, who had it restored, breaking all the rules that apply to ancient sites of this kind. He had the walls rebuilt, and here and there he had bricks inserted that bear his name.

After my tour of Babylon, I want to go to Najaf, a city that's sacred for the Shi'ites. Imam Ali, son-in-law of the Prophet Muhammad, is buried there. But Saif objects.

"What the fuck do you want to go there for? Let's go to Basra. They have great babes there. And great whorehouses; they might even have girls from your country," he says dreamily.

But I insist that I prefer Najaf to the whorehouse and the great babes. With his tail between his legs, Saif packs his nice little hipster backpack and trails after me. A few hours and more than a dozen checkpoints later, we're drinking pomegranate juice at a cheap hotel in the center of the Shi'ites' holiest city after Mecca.

The mosque that stands on the site of Ali's grave is an architectural gem. The wealth of mosaics, gold leaf, and amazing decorations and patterns is breathtaking. We watch as believers from around the world pay homage to their saint, circling his grave with prayers on their lips. As I walk around it with them, I pray for world peace. If there is an Allah somewhere in heaven, if there is a prophet Ali, maybe they'll hear me.

Everyone is here: from proud, tall Berbers from the Maghreb to small, slant-eyed oldsters from Kyrgyzstan. Now and then they come carrying a coffin, knocked together out of a few planks, and circle Ali's grave with it, because the Shi'ites want his blessing even after death. And they want to be buried as close to him as possible; the cemetery in Najaf is the world's biggest necropolis.

Hearing me talking to Saif in English, one of the security guards at the mosque comes up to us and asks where I'm from. I take the opportunity to ask him what it's like to work at this holy site.

"It's the worst after a terrorist attack," he says. "Then they bring arms, legs, torsos, all thrown into several coffins. They weep and wail, and there's dreadful chaos. It's all very depressing."

"And what was your life like in Saddam's day?" I ask.

"Dreadful." The guard sticks his fingers in his long, thick beard, as if that will help him to dredge up the memories from over twenty years ago. "Saddam was a Sunni, and he regarded us Shi'ites as the enemy. In 1980, when the war with Iran began, whatever bad thing happened, we were suspected of being behind it."

"Ayatollah Khomeini was a Shi'ite too," adds Saif. "He lived here for over a decade when the shah threw him out of Iran. It was Saddam who forced him to leave. Soon after that the revolution erupted in Iran, and Khomeini became head of state."

"Saif, how come you know that?" I ask my hipster pal.

Just a few hours ago, religion seemed to be the last thing to interest him, and suddenly he turns out to be an expert on Shia affairs.

"When I was younger, I wanted to be an imam," he admits.

It's the first time since we've known each other that he seems flustered. I think he even blushes.

Khomeini never forgave Saddam for having him thrown out of Najaf. After coming to power, Khomeini began to sponsor anyone who wanted to fight against the Iraqi government. He incited the local Shi'ites and bought weapons for the Kurds.

It was in response to his activities that in the summer of 1980 the Iraqi army attacked Iran. The Iraqi commanders were convinced the neighboring country was plunged in chaos and it would take them only a few weeks to win the war.

Except that Saddam, despite having no military experience,

wanted to make all the decisions himself. He was afraid that the charismatic generals would steal the hearts of the Iraqis, so just in case, now and then he changed commanders. He missed the moment when the road to Tehran was open to his army, and the Iranians put up a defense. Instead of being quickly over, the war became an arduous struggle for every inch of land and went on for years and years.

Horrified by Khomeini's revolution, almost the entire world supported Saddam. Weapons and instructors poured into Iraq from the United States, Western Europe, and the Soviet Union. In the cold war period, that was exceptional.

At first, Saddam showed the Iraqis a fatherly face: he paid personal visits to the widows and mothers of those killed in action, provided them with generous pensions, and bought them cars.

But the longer the conflict continued, the more he lost patience, especially when several times running the Iranians refused to agree to a peace treaty. The commanders would spend hours waiting for Saddam's decisions, but he was incapable of making them. Any attempt to desert was punished by death.

The war that cost both sides more than a million lives brought neither one victory.

18.

I don't know how it was possible, but Saddam's first wife, Sajida, didn't know about Samira for ages. Saddam was very loyal to the people who worked for him; clearly we all repaid him with the same loyalty.

But it couldn't last forever, and finally the truth came out. While her husband's affairs were one thing, marrying another woman was quite another. Islam allows it, but Sajida was furious. She stopped showing up at the farm at all. Even Uday and Qusay stopped coming there.

Apparently—I don't know this for sure, but it's what everyone was saying at the time—even Sajida's brothers were opposed to Saddam. In their view, Saddam's presidency was not just his personal achievement but that of all the al-Tikritis. Sajida was one of them, but Samira was not. They regarded marrying her as a betrayal.

And in Iraq no one forgives betrayal.

Saddam had not just the war with Iran to deal with but war with his own family too.

19.

Not long after Saddam's marriage to Samira came to light, Kamel Hana got drunk at his villa and started shooting in the air for fun. Uday's villa was a few hundred yards away. So Uday sent his bodyguards to tell him to stop.

The bodyguards weren't very successful, because Hana went on shooting. Perhaps he did it to spite Uday? They'd never liked each other; what's more, everyone knew perfectly well that it was Hana who brought Saddam women. Or maybe he was too drunk to know what he was doing? I have no idea.

Enraged, Uday drove over to Hana's house. He picked up his metal rod and started smashing Hana's car with it. Hana came running out of the house, and with all his might the furious Uday struck him on the head with the metal rod.

I had never seen Saddam cry before. But at Kamel Hana's funeral he stood in the church—because Hana was a

Christian—near his coffin, and I saw the tears streaming down his cheeks. He'd lost a good friend, someone very important to him. What's more, that friend had died at the hand of Saddam's son.

At the farm we were very upset by Kamel Hana's death. He was a likable, good man, loved by Saddam and by all of us.

Saddam sent Uday to jail, had him locked in a small cell, and forbade them to let anyone visit him. Then he went to see him, and apparently he almost killed him with his bare hands.

But his fatherly love won out, and just a few months later he released his son. He made him leave the country for a while, but we all knew that Uday was back in favor. He eventually returned, and I saw him very often after that.

20.

We made peace with Iran, but unfortunately it wasn't long before we were at war again. The Kuwaitis decided to take advantage of the fact that we were weak and had war debts, and they started selling crude oil to other countries at a much lower price than they should.

Saddam tried talking to them, to explain that we Arabs should support each other.

But it was impossible.

One day I arrived at work as usual, switched on the television, and heard that our tanks were off to war again. You ask how come I didn't know about any preparations earlier. But there's nothing odd about that. A cook isn't involved in politics. There's no country where the president asks his cook if he can start a war.

At the time, everyone said the invasion had been agreed upon with the Americans. So when the old president Bush started complaining, Saddam was furious. In the war against Iran the whole world had been on his side. He thought they'd turn a blind eye this time too.

He was wrong.

The Americans were actually on Kuwait's side, and our troops were forced to withdraw. Later, Bush launched an invasion of Iraq, and that was when the situation became dangerous. I didn't see Saddam for weeks on end, although I know he was in Baghdad. He went into hiding at various houses and apartments, downtown as well as on the outskirts of the city. It looked as if the Americans would enter the capital and try to kill him.

In the kitchen, too, a lot of things changed. We went on cooking as usual, but Saddam didn't eat at home. Every day one of his bodyguards would come and take his meals to him.

But there were also days when they took us somewhere, a different place each time, and told us to do the cooking there. Later, when the Americans were outside Baghdad and the bombing began, they transferred us to the Amariya district. We had a rented house there where we cooked, and once again someone came and took the food to Saddam. I didn't see the president for several months.

Later, the Americans withdrew and the sanctions remained.

People sometimes say that because of the sanctions Saddam had to eat worse food because lots of items couldn't be bought in Iraq. That's not true. He ate just as before. He had never eaten imported foods; he ate only Iraqi dishes, made exclusively from Iraqi produce. Why would he eat imported rice when we have the world's best rice here in Iraq? The amber variety, which grows near Najaf, is superior to any rice you can buy in Asia.

What would we have bought abroad? Meat? That's hard for me to imagine, because our butcher killed a fresh goat or sheep for us every day. Fish? The best fish is here in Iraq. *Mazgouf*, his favorite fish, is a species you can find only in Iraq.

Saddam was very fond of fish, barbecued food, soups, kebabs, and shawarma. He liked zucchini soup, lentil soup, and soup made of okra, otherwise known as ladies' fingers. All these things grew in Iraq; what's more, they grew on our farm, right under our noses. How could the sanctions change anything?

The sanctions affected ordinary Iraqis worst of all. They were the ones who stopped earning as much as they had in the past. They're still feeling the burden of those unfair sanctions to this day.

21.

Most of the experts on Middle Eastern affairs agree that the Americans could have deposed Saddam in 1991 without much trouble. They had three-quarters of the country on their side, including the Shi'ites and the Kurds, who had been inciting anti-Saddam insurgencies.

But when the Americans withdrew without deposing him, Saddam took cruel revenge. General al-Majid, who had used chemical weapons against the Kurds, killed tens of thousands of people. From a beautiful, rich country, Iraq became a ruin.

While the Iraqis were starving, their president began a major palace-construction program. The best architects, the best interior decorators, and the best painters and sculptors were enlisted for the job. Several dozen palaces were built throughout the country. They were meant to be a way of giving the finger to those around the world who had declared economic war on Iraq.

I'm touring one of these palaces in Hillah, the city adjacent to the ruins of ancient Babylon, with Saif. Everything that could be removed from this residence ended up in the homes of the local residents long ago, but even so we're stunned by the opulence of the decor. From the entrance on, the palace is dripping with expensive mosaics, and the walls and floors are covered in marble. In the garden, among the orange trees, Saddam had a pool with a view of the river Tigris; there had to be a pool of this kind at every one of his palaces.

Upstairs, there's an unexpected souvenir from the days when the Poles took part in George H. W. Bush's infamous Iraqi coalition. There's an entire wall splattered with hearts featuring the names of Polish boys and girls: Sławek loves Marta, Jacek loves Ilona, and Zbyszek loves Marzena. In another room half the wall is covered in hearts for the Great Orchestra of Christmas Charity; the Polish soldiers in Iraq were collecting for this organization, which funds hospital equipment for newborn babies and others.

While we're touring the palace, a man named Mohammed approaches us. The skin on his face is blighted by smallpox scars, and he has a jaunty little mustache that takes a few years off him.

"I worked at this palace as a guard," he says, and smiles under his mustache.

Then he adds that for a little baksheesh he'd be happy to show us around. So I ask him to help us to find the kitchen. And—if possible—the cook who worked here.

"There were two cooks. One left Hillah, and the other is dead," says Mohammed. "But I know where the kitchen is."

He leads us down some wide stairs, located just behind the pool, into the basement. I don't think anyone has been down here for ages, because there are bits of stone wall, dust, and bat droppings scattered all over the floor.

"Those cooks had the strangest job in the world," says our guide on the way. "Every day they made breakfast, lunch, and dinner, just as if Saddam were here. They had to leave samples of the food in the fridge, as though it were going to be tested for poison. And then at night they threw everything they'd made into the trash."

"Why did they do that?" I ask.

"For safety reasons. Saddam built lots of palaces so no one would ever find out which one he happened to be staying in. He could have been at any of them. So the staff worked at each one as if he were there. Sometimes he sent out a column of empty cars so his enemies would think he was going somewhere. Those columns used to come here too."

"But why did they throw the food away?"

"It was the president's food, meant for him alone. No one else was allowed to touch it. There was a great deal of that food, and one day some of the indigent locals found the site where it was thrown away. They started going there to collect it, but a few days later they were all arrested and beaten up."

Mohammed finally locates Saddam's kitchen for us. We tour it in the dark, lighting our way with our cell phones. There's no trace of any kitchen equipment left, just a large ventilation shaft running up the wall and ceiling. In fact, other than this solid aluminum structure, there's nothing here at all.

"Did Saddam ever eat anything prepared by these cooks?"

"He was only at this palace twice," says Mohammed. "But he came with his own cooks. The entire local staff were locked in a room and forbidden to come out."

22.

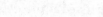

After the war with Kuwait, I was feeling very tired of working for the president. The worst thing was the unpredictability. That finished me off.

I waited for the right moment, and finally I told one of his bodyguards that I wanted to leave.

Saddam summoned me. "I've heard you want to leave me."

I said I was sorry, but it was true.

The president nodded.

"All right. I understand."

A few weeks later my great dream finally came true, and I started working at a five-star hotel called the Tala. When I left Saddam's service, the administration had only one request. Saddam loved my *bastirma*, which is dried beef. He asked me to come and make it for him once a year; *bastirma* is always made in the winter.

I agreed without hesitation, and for several years I took an annual vacation, ordered all the ingredients, and made one and a half or two tons of it, enough to supply the palace for the next twelve months. Saddam never stopped being generous, and while he was in power, he went on paying me a monthly salary, as if I were still working for him.

A few years after I left the job, Osama bin Laden sent two jets to destroy the Twin Towers in New York. Straight after that, George W. Bush declared that his greatest enemy in the entire world was Saddam Hussein.

You know the rest.

Uday and Qusay were killed in Mosul, shot by the Americans.

Samira and Sajida both left Iraq, each in a different direction. I don't know where they are, but I bet Saddam made sure that neither of them would suffer in poverty.

Saddam was hanged.

I made my last *bastirma* shortly before the second American attack. When they caught the president at a house in the suburbs of Tikrit, they found some of that food draped on the palm trees. He had it with him to the end.

23.

When the Americans captured Baghdad, I was terrified. They were looking for people who had worked for Saddam. I was afraid they'd take me to Guantánamo and kill me or torture me.

We all went into hiding, each of us as best he could. They didn't find any of the old team of cooks. The only person I worked with who was arrested was a man who used to come to the palace to change the batteries in the television remote controls and repair the TV sets. Later, I found out they were looking for information on how Saddam lived so they could use it to catch him. They clearly found someone, but who could it have been? I have no idea. Toward the end there were only al-Tikritis left in Saddam's entourage.

After fifteen years in the job I had a lot of pictures of Saddam, taken at various moments. As I told you, he loved being photographed, and later his photographer brought me the pictures. When the Americans invaded, I was so scared that I hid them all under the air conditioner.

Several months later the situation stabilized, and it occurred to me that by now the worst was behind us. But there was water leaking from the air conditioner, and everything I'd hidden under it was ruined, including all the photos, apart from one. Look, I've brought it to show you. I remember the moment it was taken—on the road between Tikrit, Saddam's hometown, and Samarra, the city where one of the oldest mosques in Iraq is located. We had stopped somewhere in the fields for lunch. Saddam ate his food, and he liked it, so then he said, "Abu Ali, you're a real master. Let's take a picture."

It was a beautiful, sunny day; we were all in a good mood. Here, take a look. It's the only one I have left after all these years.

Snack

At first my cooking was very bad. When I think back to my first days in the kitchen, I feel a bit ashamed.

But there's something you have to know about Pol Pot. He had an incredible sense of humor. He was like a clown, he really was. From my first encounters with him I remember that he was handsome and had a beautiful smile, but I also remember that he was always joking.

His favorite joke was to say the opposite of what he meant. For instance, if he thought I'd made too much food, he'd say, "Oh dear, how little food our Moeun has made. We're all going to starve." And he'd look me in the eyes, waiting to see how I'd respond, and smile his amazing smile. And when in the first months I made soup for him, sometimes he'd rub his stomach and say, "Wonderful soup." And I never knew if he was joking or he really meant it.

Only in time did I realize that he was in fact joking. And that I still had a lot to learn before I could cook well.

So I learned. For all our sakes, it was very important for Brother Pouk to be well fed. Our lives depended on him having enough to eat. The success of our revolution depended on it.

Every day I cooked a few things that I knew he liked. Fish,

papaya salad, chicken. He always chooses one of those, I thought. The main thing was for him to eat his fill. It was all the more important because he often had a stomachache that prevented him from sleeping at night.

So I made a lot of food. He'd see the table laden with food and say with a smile, "Oh dear, how little food our Moeun has made . . . What a lazy girl."

And he'd smile at me again.

Lunch
Chiemo

Roasted Goat

The Story of Otonde Odera,
Idi Amin's Chef

1.

First of all, brother, tell me, do you believe in God? Do you believe in Jesus Christ, who gave his life for our salvation?

Brother, if it is as you say, let us shake hands and pray together. Let us pray, as in the days of the apostles.

Dear Lord, by whose will and grace we are all alive, who saved me from being attacked by the hyenas and the hippopotamus, who snatched me from the hands of Idi Amin's assassins just as they were dragging me away to their dungeons to meet my death; O God, who is looking down on us at this very moment, who is watching us when we laugh and when we cry, and who places the food on our table—bread and fish, as in the time of our Lord Jesus Christ, as well as rice, chicken Kiev, and carrots—let us thank you for all your gifts. Let us thank you for the guests who have come to hear the story of my extraordinary life.

O God, who has given so much to me—a boy from the village of Rambugu on the shore of the Great Lake, a poor Luo, though he never finished a single class at school, who was never even enrolled at any school, whose mother earned a living by doing laundry for her richer neighbors and never thought that one day she would sleep in an expensive hotel, that she would travel to foreign countries, who could never have imagined that her son would cook for presidents, that he would fly abroad in an airplane, that he would shake the hands of the first black leaders of all the African countries, and that they would shake his hand and call him "brother"— although You gave me all this, including cars and good clothing, later, from one day to the next, You took everything away from me, to show me that nothing in this world is certain apart from Your love, dear Lord, king of kings, we praise You and worship You.

2.

At first light we set off from Kisumu, the third-largest city in Kenya, where shoelace sellers and packs of stray dogs wander the streets, and where the drivers of the motorcycle taxis that are known here as *boda bodas* wait for customers. We drive along the shore of Lake Victoria, as vast as the sea and as unsettling as death, its waves capable of turning a fishing boat belly up. With me are Julia Prus, the Africa correspondent for Polish Radio, and Carl Odera, a local journalist who comes from the same tribe as the cook whom we are on our way to see (they even have the same last name, but they're not related).

We're going to meet the man who cooked for Idi Amin, the Ugandan dictator who had his enemies thrown to the crocodiles.

We pass boats painted yellow, green, blue, and black, decorated with images of popular politicians, TV stars, or Jesus Christ the Savior. Finally, we reach a village where the earth is red brown, the color of clotted blood. Here we turn off and drive for some time along a blood-red road, before making another turn, then a third one, and a fourth. The birds are singing madly as the thorny branches of trees scrape the side of the car. We drive down a steep hill and park under a tall tree, under which a man who looks like a biblical patriarch is sitting on an old orange box, surrounded by his family. He's tall and thin, like the grass growing on the savanna; he has prominent cheekbones, and as we come closer, I see that he also has long, thin fingers with large fingernails. As I approach the tree, he gets up and embraces me, and instantly I feel as if I've found a long-lost friend.

The man who looks like a patriarch is Otonde Odera. Those great long fingers of his have diced meat and vegetables and ground rice for two Ugandan presidents in succession, including Idi Amin, the bloody dictator said by some to have eaten human flesh.

Did Otonde ever cook it for Amin? How did he prepare it? What did he serve with it?

And how do you go on living after something like that?

I want to ask him those questions. But how?

I don't know. Not yet. And I haven't time to stop to think about it, because at once Odera leads me to the house, where on a wall, under a one-string fiddle, hangs a black-and-white photograph of a woman.

It's his mother.

It was from her that it all began, so if our conversation is to go according to the will of God, we must start from her too. And from an incident that marked this man for his entire life.

3.

My mother's name was Teresa Anaza, and my father's was Odera Ojode. My mother had thirteen children before me, but they all died in turn. Smallpox, malaria, whooping cough. My parents were very poor; they couldn't afford a doctor.

Nobody expected me to survive either. My mother already had a very large belly when she went to visit her sister. My aunt's husband, Nyangoma Obiero, was a fisherman, and they lived right on the shore of the lake, in the village of Liunda. Sometimes my uncle gave my parents fish. Every few weeks my mother went to see them.

From our house it takes a good few hours to walk to the lake, but Momma didn't want to stay the night there, so although dusk was falling, she set off on the return journey. "Don't go," they told her. "There are lots of hyenas along the road." Just a few days earlier they had bitten a man very badly.

But my mother was adamant. And when she insisted, it was impossible to persuade her to change her mind. She said goodbye, hugged my aunt, picked up her bundle of fish, and went on her way.

On and on she walked, until the sun had set behind the lake and the temperature grew cooler. Soon night fell, but she kept walking.

Roughly halfway home, she started to feel unwell. She had given birth to thirteen babies before me, so she must have known what was about to happen.

She found a good spot not far from the road. She lay down on the ground. She was stuck in the middle of a field, all alone, far away from any other people. She tensed her muscles. Then the top of my head appeared. She tensed again. And the birth was over. Giving birth to your fourteenth child is a much easier process.

Then my mother picked a sharp blade of grass and cut the umbilical cord with it. Then she pulled a cactus from the ground, laid the placenta in the hole where its roots had been, wrapped me in the placenta, and sat down beside me.

She could hear the hyenas howling in the distance. She was sure they'd smell the blood and come for us. Later in life, she told me many times how she had waited for death. My death. And hers too. She'd already survived so many difficult times by then that she was ready for it.

But although the hyenas spent the whole night circling us, they didn't approach.

And I didn't die.

As soon as the sun rose, my mother wrapped me in some rags and headed for the village. When she got there, nobody could believe she had come back with a live baby. Everyone came running to our house, including a wise old man who knew how to heal and could predict the future. And he said, "If the hyenas won't touch him, he'll live a very long time."

The old man was right. Look, I'm eighty years old now, and my life has been long enough for ten other people to share it with me.

4.

We lived poorly, but I can't remember us ever going hungry. We usually ate manioc, or manioc flour with a vegetable of some kind. Meat was an extreme rarity. My father always had two or three cows, but if he did slaughter one of them, all the meat went to the market. We needed the money to pay our debts; we always owed our neighbors for something.

The food eaten by the Luo, the tribe I am from, is quite like the food of the *mzungu*, the white people. The main ingredients are cooked vegetables or meat. The *mzungu* eat potatoes; we eat manioc, buckwheat, or rice. Except that it's not enough for the *mzungu* to have a little buckwheat or manioc, and a small piece of meat; the *mzungu* have to bake cheese too, put it on their vegetables, and stew the meat in wine first. *Mzungu* cuisine is the food of people who want to show that they have power. Because food is power. I learned that from cooking for presidents. If you have food, you also have women, you have money, you have people's admiration. You can have whatever you want.

Our food is the food of people who know what hunger is. We have nothing to prove to anyone. We eat to have the strength to go on working.

While I was living with my parents, I had various occupations. First I dabbled in music; I played the *orutu*, a kind of fiddle that's popular among people from the Luo tribe. It has one string, and you play it with a bow, resting the instrument against your hip. I used to earn money playing it at weddings and other special events.

Then my uncle took me out on his boat to be a fisherman. I sailed with him for about two years.

Until one day a hippopotamus attacked our boat. We saw it from afar, swimming toward us. An angry hippo is much worse than a crocodile: it moves very fast in the water. It swam up and overturned our boat, sending us all flying helplessly in different directions. It's a miracle no harm came to anyone that day, because that hippo had already killed several people, and all the fishermen around the lake were afraid of it.

After the hippo attack I said to my uncle, "I wasn't the only one of fourteen siblings to survive just to die now if it comes back."

My uncle agreed with me. One of his sons, Sylvester, was working in Kampala, in Uganda, at a club that was popular with the *mzungu*. My uncle said I should take the boat to Kampala and find the club, and his son would be sure to help me to find a job.

For us, the Luo, family ties are very important. Did you know that the former American president Barack Obama is Luo too? His father comes from a village twelve miles from here. And even though he has never lived here, Obama often helps his family in any way he can. So I knew that Sylvester would not refuse to help me.

I boarded the boat from Kisumu to Entebbe, and as soon as it docked, I went straight to my cousin.

The "Kampala" club was a very important place for the *mzungu*, because most of the people sent by the British government to work in Uganda spent their first few weeks living in the hotel next to it, until a suitable rental home was found for them. My cousin was a groundskeeper there and swept the floors. He was very pleased to see me and went straight to the manager and instantly got me a job as a waiter's assistant. I didn't know a word of English, but luckily it wasn't necessary. All I had to do was smile and carry food from the kitchen to the dining room.

What about the hippopotamus, you ask? One day it simply disappeared. People say it must have been the spirit of a warrior who had come to take revenge on his enemies.

5.

To find out more about the Luo tribe, Julia, Carl, and I go to see its senior matriarch, Mama Sarah Obama, a ninety-five-year-old philanthropist famous for her fight against AIDS and for raising money for the education of children from the local villages. Her village, Kogelo, is a stone's throw from Otonde Odera's house. It is from here that Barack Obama Sr. set off to study in the United States.

We are admitted into the grounds of the property by a security guard employed by the Kenyan government; he doesn't only work here, but he and his entire family live in a cabin right by the entrance gate. He checks our documents and asks about the purpose of our visit to Mama Sarah before pointing out the site of the Obama family's ancestral graves, where the father and grandfather of the forty-fourth president of the United States are buried.

I go to pay my respects to them.

Beside the plain terrazzo slabs covering the earthly remains of the president's honorable forebears, two black-and-white cows are grazing. There's another one mooing in a barn nearby; two days ago she gave birth to her first calf, and she's probably not over the shock yet. Hens run between our legs and butterflies whirl overhead. The Obama clan's place of origin is sleepy and pastoral.

Mama Sarah has just awoken from her postprandial nap. She puts on an African print dress and receives us on the porch. She was the third wife of Hussein Onyango Obama, President Obama's grandfather. Although they don't have the same blood running in their veins, he still addresses her as "Granny."

"My husband was much older than me," she says. "I was nineteen when we married, and he was over forty. That's what times were like then. A girl did not choose her own husband. The *jagam*, or matchmaker, came to the house and said to her parents, 'Such and such a man is interested in your daughter. What do you say?'

"It was 1941, and the people in this region of Kenya had only seen their first airplane a few years earlier. In Luo, the language of our tribe, they called it *dege*, and at once in every other family, as soon as a child was born, they named it Dege too. In honor of the airplane, for being such an extraordinary invention. When the first spoons appeared, children were named after them too: Ojiko. Or Asande, in honor of the plate.

"But that doesn't mean the Luo were poorly educated. On the contrary. They're regarded as the best-educated tribe in all of East Africa. As soon as one of them has money, he doesn't buy himself a car or gold, but at once he considers which school to send his child to. When you were on your way to see me, you saw children in school uniforms, didn't you? They all go to school. The Luo are hungry for knowledge.

"And that's what my husband did. He sent his children to America to be educated there. Barack wouldn't have risen so high if not for the fact that the Luo care about education.

"I had a very good life with my husband, and to this day I believe that no one can make a better suggestion of whom to marry than a matchmaker. Indeed, Obama was older, indeed, I was his third wife, but he looked great and he was in good shape. So we had a good life, but no one is going to live forever. And for almost forty years I have been on my own.

"But wait a moment . . . There's something I don't understand."
At this point Barack Obama's adopted grandma pauses dramatically. "Why are you asking questions about my late husband? Are
you going to propose to me?"

6.

The sun is gradually setting over Otonde Odera's house, so we move
from under the old tree into the cottage. It's made of brick, fired
from the local clay, whose blood-red shade, once it has dried in the
sun, changes to a creamy brown. The walls of the building are
cracked, and through the chinks the entire vicinity is clearly visible. Every gust of wind of more than average strength makes the
tin roof rattle, as if it were about to fall on our heads.

But it doesn't.

We sit around a small table drinking chai, which is what they
call tea here, and continue to listen to Otonde.

I liked working at the club, and because I'm very hardworking
by nature, whenever I had free time, I assisted the others. I'd
carry someone's suitcase, help with the cleaning, or change a
broken lightbulb in a hotel room. I was popular, and after a
few months a *mzungu* couple, Mr. and Mrs. Robertson, asked
if I would like to change my job and come to work for them as
a shamba boy—meaning a gardener.

For a young man like me, to be a shamba boy, or just "boy"
for short, because that's what young men working in *mzungu*
homes were called, was like a kiss from God. So I agreed without hesitation. I moved to the Robertsons' and settled in the

gardener's cottage, right next to their house, and every day I took care of mowing the lawn. For some reason the *mzungu* grass must grow as if measured with a ruler. None of us would have been worried about it, because we have far bigger problems to deal with than cutting the grass. But for the *mzungu* it was a matter requiring the employment of an extra person—me—and constant instruction and correction.

I addressed Mr. Robertson like that, "Mr. Robertson." But his wife preferred me to call her Memsahib. That's what we called women from Britain; the man was Sahib, and the woman was Memsahib. As a result, although I owe her a great deal, I cannot remember her first name.

Once I had learned to cut the grass properly, it turned out I had a lot of spare time. Then the memsahib started asking me to help her with the cleaning. So I washed the steps, cleaned the windows, and swept the kitchen floor. And when it turned out I could do all that and still had time to spare—all my life I've been a very hard worker—the memsahib said I was to help her in the kitchen.

And that's how it all began.

It was like magic. As if I'd found exactly what I should be doing all my life. I can't remember what the memsahib first instructed me to do. Maybe it was cutting up meat to make chops? Maybe it was kneading dough? Or chopping carrots for the salad? I don't know, I can't remember. It must have been something simple; I had no idea how to move without breaking things.

But right from the start I felt as if I were born in the kitchen. As if I had found something that God wanted me to do; he had chosen it for me long before I was born.

The memsahib couldn't believe how quickly I learned to do various things. One day she showed me the right way to hold a knife, and a few hours later I was chopping things up very skillfully. Another time I watched as she made and baked pastry; the next day I was able to bake it the same way. Once we cooked T-bone steak together, and the next day I knew how to do it all on my own. And the T-bone is a very difficult steak: it has sirloin steak on one side and rump on the other, divided by the vertebrae. You grill rump steak one way, and sirloin another, so it's quite complicated, and I tell you, to this day I don't know how I caught on to it all without knowing a word of English.

I never made notes; writing wasn't and still isn't my strong suit. But that meant I learned even more quickly; I knew I had to memorize it all. Later, when I was in charge of the kitchen at the presidential palace, I did the shopping for more than a hundred people without making any notes. I was capable of buying a hundred chickens and ten goats for a reception, selecting the vegetables and spices to go with them, and keeping the list in my head, including the soup and the dessert. And everything always worked out perfectly.

Every day the memsahib taught me something new. She was very happy to see how well I coped with the cooking. Finding a gardener or someone to do the cleaning was no problem for the *mzungu*. But finding someone who could cook the way they liked it was close to a miracle. The richest people brought their cooks with them, from England. The Robertsons weren't quite so rich, so as soon as I turned out to have golden hands in the kitchen, the memsahib ran to her husband.

Mr. Robertson nodded to say yes. From then on I stopped being a gardener, and they employed another boy in my place. I, Otonde Odera, a boy from a small village, who had almost been eaten by hyenas immediately after his birth, became the cook for white people.

It was a great distinction. After all, a cook might not wash his hands and could poison you, so you have to trust him very much to be sure he's clean and does everything as he should. Not many blacks succeeded in gaining that sort of trust from the *mzungu*, so I never forgot that I must always have clean hands. And a clean, laundered apron. That was when I drummed it into my head that whatever happens, a cook must look neat and tidy.

The memsahib taught me everything. How to roast a chicken. How to cook fish. How to tell if the meat is ready to come out of the frying pan. Do you know? While it's still sizzling, it's all right. If it stops sizzling, that means it has soaked up all the oil and it won't taste good.

After about a year, the memsahib showed me through sign language that now she could leave me in the kitchen on my own and that I didn't need her help for the daily cooking, or for making the pastries, or for baking Indian chapati bread, which they adored.

I learned to cook very well, but I never learned to speak English. Of course I knew a few words: "roast," "melted," "boil," "cook." And that's all. Nothing else.

But I didn't need more English than that. The white man didn't want the black man to discuss what it said in the newspapers with him. The white man wanted to have a neatly cut lawn, a thoroughly washed floor, and tasty food.

That suited me. I didn't want to hold conversations with the memsahib and her husband either. I knew I was the kitchen boy, it gave me immense pleasure, and if I had had to talk, I'd have been afraid of saying the wrong thing, or of saying one word too many, and then they'd throw me out of the job.

That's what I learned in the white man's house. To wash my hands, dress well, and never say too much, because no one expects the cook to have opinions.

7.

Once I felt that I had a steady job and my life was good, I decided to invite a woman to share it with me.

Every few months I went back to Kenya, to visit my family. On one of these trips I was invited to the wedding of one of my cousins. There I met Elizabeth, a girl from the village of Aluor, about ten miles from my village. She was slim, with lovely eyes and a long neck. I immediately found her attractive. Two months after my cousin's wedding we were married too. I had to buy her parents a cow before they'd agree to let me marry her. They wanted two and weren't very pleased when I only offered them one; Elizabeth was a beautiful girl, and it was clear that if not I, then another man would soon try to win her. But someone explained to them that I was working abroad, for *mzungu*, and that I was a better match than the local boys, even if one of them were to give them two cows.

That persuaded them.

Elizabeth went on living in Kenya, while I lived in Uganda, so every few months I went to see her, bringing presents— earrings, clothes, but also more practical things, such as cooking pots. I wanted to take her home with me, but I didn't have the courage to ask the memsahib if I could bring my wife to live with me in the cottage next to their house.

Later there was no opportunity to do that.

The whites in Uganda were starting to have more and more problems. Mr. Robertson, who worked for the British government, was often anxious.

It wasn't a good moment to bring my wife to Kampala.

8.

Mr. Robertson had reasons to be anxious.

Since the end of World War II, Africa had been in a state of independence fever. Until then, people of his kind, employees of the colonial powers, had lived like *mandazi*—Ugandan donuts—in sweet syrup. There they were paid far more than they would have received in their home countries. Even middle-ranking employees could afford to rent large houses and to employ servants. Now they'd have to find another way to earn a living. "Following World War II, Europe wanted to give up its colonies. France and Great Britain regarded colonialism as a costly anachronism," says the Polish foreign correspondent Wojciech Jagielski, a specialist on Africa.

For centuries the Africans had been debased by the Europeans, sold as slaves, exploited, and treated as second-class human beings.

Now they suddenly had to take African affairs into their own hands.

In 1951, Libya declared independence.

In 1956, it was followed by Sudan, Tunisia, and Morocco.

In 1957, it was Ghana's turn.

In 1958, it was Guinea's.

Then the process picked up speed. The real watershed came in 1960, when as many as sixteen African countries declared independence.

"The colonial powers said goodbye to Africa in a hurry, without preparing it for independence. Weak, independent African countries would be easier prey for exploitation than colonies pressing their claims," says Jagielski.

On October 9, 1962, at a grand ceremony, Uganda, too, declared independence.

9.

Otonde Odera and I are off to the market in Kisumu to buy food to cook together. We wade up to our knees in green leaves, in tomatoes as red as the sun setting over the savanna, and in chili peppers ranging from the hottest to the mildest.

There's an infinite range of fruits and vegetables on sale here— delicious bananas display their curves, pineapples puff out their armored chests, and mangoes and papayas emit their tempting aromas.

Later we go across to the meat section of the bazaar. It's easy to find: we're led there by the loud buzzing of flies. The butchers, who wear regulation Muslim caps and neatly trimmed beards, are happy to offer advice. But Otonde doesn't need advice. He chooses the best chicken, to his mind—not too fat, but not too stringy either.

"I'd have chosen one just like that for Amin," he says, because I have asked him to make me dinner exactly the way he made it for the dictator.

Finally, we come to the fishmongers, from whom we buy a medium-sized tilapia, the most common Lake Victoria fish.

We have everything. We can return to the village, where outside his house, over an open hearth, Odera sets up a camp stove and—like an officer giving orders to his soldiers—assigns culinary tasks to his daughter-in-law and his two little granddaughters.

The chicken is roasting over a bonfire. The fish is sizzling in the frying pan. The women are taking care of the vegetables.

We can go back to our conversation.

10.

Imagine the following situation: all the people around me were happy; they were singing and drinking banana beer.

Only I was sad.

That's what happened when Uganda declared independence and the whites left the country. Almost all the blacks were saying, "At last our country will be just for us! At last the *mzungu* won't be telling us what to do!"

But I was left without a job and with no hope of being able to bring my wife, Elizabeth, to Uganda. All I had were my two hands and my willingness to work.

And my skills.

Then someone told me that the administration of Milton Obote, the prime minister of Uganda, was looking for a kitchen worker. I thought, "I'm the ideal candidate!"

So I went to the prime minister's office. At the beginning of independence it was like that. If you had a question for the prime minister or another minister, you just came and told them what it was about. That was supposed to distinguish the government of Africans from the government of the *mzungu*, who often refused to listen to us.

There they asked me what dishes I was able to cook. I listed them. They nodded and invited me to come back in a few days' time for an exam.

So I went.

The first part of the exam was a conversation. There were several people listening, including the chief of administration, Oyite Ojok, who—as I later learned—had a favorite, a man from his village whom he wanted to employ.

After the conversation came the practical exam. We had to make oxtail soup, T-bone steak for the main course, and a dried fruit pudding for dessert.

Oxtail is a delicacy, so you have to know how to cook it properly. I took two oxtails, boiled them, and added carrot, parsley, and seasoning—allspice and pepper. After half an hour I removed the tails, stripped the meat off them, added diced potato, and it was done.

The T-bone steak is very difficult, as I've already told you: it is rump and sirloin, two different kinds of meat, in a single steak.

Luckily, I had made both dishes with the memsahib. Mr. Robertson was particularly fond of steak, so I had mastered the T-bone to perfection.

Dried fruit pudding is also quite hard to make. The sauce contains many ingredients: apricots, pears, apples, and other fruits. You mix them all together, bake them at a low temperature, then add cinnamon, cream, vanilla, wine, pomegranate seeds, and finally walnuts or hazelnuts. It tastes like cake, alcohol, and nuts all at once. If it's well made, it's delicious. And luckily for me, I had it down to a fine art.

A few days passed, and I went to hear the answer.

"You start work tomorrow," they said.

Only then did I realize what I was getting into. The prime minister. Oh my goodness!

Obote chose me because very few blacks knew how to cook food for whites. Those who could already had jobs—they worked at the best hotels—and didn't want to swap them for employment at the prime minister's office, for an unknown fee. Obote had become fond of *mzungu* cuisine and wanted to have the dishes he'd grown used to in the colonial era. Independence was one thing, but he wasn't going to change his diet. Funny, isn't it? A black prime minister employs a chef who's black but who knows how to cook for whites.

The fact that I am Luo also meant a lot. Obote was from the Lango tribe, and the Lango are our brothers. Obote's administration employed a large number of people from my region. I did wonder why. I think they saw us a bit like mercenaries: you people are not interested in who rules Uganda or in what sorts of political parties they have there. You're not going to try to poison anyone or conspire against anyone. You just want to earn a living.

I particularly liked Solomon Okuku, the prime minister's chauffeur, who was raised about ten miles from my village. Almost every day after work we sat down for a beer and chatted—about our wives, about work, about politics. We became firm friends. Okuku was kind and dedicated. But later, that would destroy him.

I also liked Odero Osore, who was the prime minister's

valet; he took care of his bed linen, ironed his clothes, and polished his shoes. Osore was from the same region as Okuku and I were, but he was more reserved than Okuku. Sometimes he chatted with us, and sometimes he had a sip of beer, but he didn't share his troubles.

It didn't bother us. Everyone has the right to keep things to themselves. We were friends; we helped each other. What more do you need?

Only the chief of administration, Oyite Ojok, was not pleased that his friend from the village had lost the competition to be the cook. He wasn't in a position to argue about it; the prime minister had the last word. But he never forgot.

11.

The fact that little Milton Obote, future prime minister and president of Uganda, survived childhood—as in the case of his cook—bordered on a miracle. One time he narrowly escaped being eaten by leopards. Another time, while racing through the jungle, he almost ran into a hunting cobra. Yet another time, a crocodile seized a little girl standing right beside him on the riverbank.

One of his grandfathers was a tribal chief, highly mistrustful of the British. The other was an herbalist who treated animals and could make it rain by magic. Milton was the apple of both grandfathers' eyes.

At roughly the same time, a little farther south in Uganda, near the barracks in a town called Jinja, another boy was kicking his heels: strong, very tall, and with no occupation. For people like him there was no work in Uganda. His name was Idi Amin.

His mother earned a living by cooking and casting spells. After breaking up with his father, she met Yafesi Yasin, a corporal in the British colonial regiment, the King's African Rifles, almost twenty years her junior. He became her partner.

Living next to the barracks had a tremendous influence on Idi's fortunes. Thanks to his strength he was quickly noticed by the army recruitment officers. That was how his career began.

For many years, Major Iain Grahame was Amin's superior officer in the King's African Rifles. With my translator and friend, Antonia Lloyd-Jones, I went to visit him at his home in East Anglia. First he showed us a mounted antelope head gifted him by Amin. Then he sat us in armchairs in the conservatory and told us, "You meet people in life who are born leaders of men ... it's a very rare thing ... and Amin was a born leader of men. But of course coupled with that was very low schooling."

Amin had always been bigger and stronger than anyone else; several times he won boxing championships in Uganda.

He also proved to be an obedient soldier, and it gave him great satisfaction to carry out an order well. Some sources say he completed only four years at elementary school, while others say he never spent a single day at school. Major Grahame recalled helping him to open a bank account. The future president spent twenty minutes trying to sign his own name.

But it didn't bother the British—on the contrary. They thought Amin seemed rather dim-witted, but he looked up to them and would be useful when Uganda declared independence.

The fact that Obote graduated from school also borders on the miraculous. He was helped by a coincidence. When he was seven years old, a soldier on leave taught him the alphabet. The boy absorbed it instantly; the very next day he picked up a book and, letter by letter, tried to decipher it. Astonished, his parents decided that such a talented child deserved the chance to be educated, and sent him to school in Kenya.

He came back a mature man and was almost immediately selected for the Uganda Legislative Council.

At the time, Idi Amin was still fighting fiercely against enemies of the British Empire.

Milton Obote soon became one of the pillars of Ugandan independence. Before the first elections he formed an alliance with the kabaka, or king of Buganda, the largest and strongest of the traditional tribal kingdoms. As a result, the kabaka became the first president of independent Uganda, and Milton Obote was its prime minister.

But half a pace behind them walked Idi Amin, the ambitious deputy head of the army, who had loyally served the British and their generals to the end.

12.

For the first few weeks I didn't meet the prime minister in person. It was a very difficult time; things were constantly happening that demanded his attention. Until one day the chief of administration, Ojok, finally summoned me to his office and introduced me: "Mr. Prime Minister, this is Otonde, the cook."

Obote was reading the newspaper. He just looked up and glanced at me for a moment. "Goood," he said, and then went on reading. My audience with him was over.

Only later did I learn that "goood" was the greatest compliment he ever paid anyone.

We left the room, and I tried to find out why the prime minister had asked about me. For a long time Ojok refused to tell me, until finally he forced himself to say that the prime minister liked my food very much. And that recently he had asked to be served only the things that I prepared.

There were several other cooks working for Obote already, all better educated than I was. The kitchen was a hotbed of ambition, with each of them wanting to be his favorite. When it turned out that Obote liked my dishes the best, the other cooks started saying nasty things about me behind my back. Tough: I just had to live with it.

Though Obote soon came to love me like a brother.

He had a special bell to order something from the kitchen. He'd ring it, and if it wasn't me who came to answer, but someone else, he'd say, "What are you doing here? I want Otonde to come."

So I'd go to him, even if I was in the middle of chopping the meat. I'd change into a clean apron, wipe my hands on a cloth, and run, as I once used to run to the memsahib. And without even looking up from his newspaper, he'd say, "Chai." Tea. So I'd bring him hot tea, but I had a special touch that no one else had thought of. In the morning, as soon as I started work, I'd bake some shortbread cookies. Small ones, perfect with a cup of tea. So whenever the prime minister asked me for tea, I'd bring him a cup and also some delicious, fresh biscuits on a small plate. That was my trademark: don't just do as they've asked, but try to anticipate what they're going to need before they ask. That saved me work, because I didn't have to take off my apron again five minutes later, wipe my hands, and run back to him with something sweet. Or waste half an hour baking cookies in the middle of the day.

Everyone was afraid of him, because he could get terribly upset if something didn't go his way. I alone was not afraid. I knew I was good at my job, that I had golden hands, and that the prime minister was not going to fire me without cause.

I had only one problem with Obote. He was stingy, even though he didn't pay for anything with his own private money. For the first few months I worked without any compensation. I told the chief of administration about it, but because he didn't like me, I don't think he passed the message on.

But finally, after several months, someone told Obote about it. And he gave orders for me to be paid 390 East African shillings per month.* It wasn't much; I think in today's money it would be a hundred dollars. But at last I was getting some cash, and I felt confident enough to bring Elizabeth to Uganda. She came to live with me in the building for employees, not far from the prime minister's headquarters.

Those first few years of ours in Kampala were beautiful. For the first time I felt like a serious man. I had a job, working for the prime minister himself. I had two good friends, Okuku and Osore. I had a wife who was living with me. Soon after, our first son, Edward, was born. I thought life would keep getting better.

---

* The currency used until the 1970s in Tanzania, Kenya, and Uganda.

13.

In 1963, an extra person came to us to be fed when Obote married a girl named Miria, who was very beautiful, with skin the color of milky coffee. Unfortunately Miria did not like the fact that I was on such good terms with the prime minister. She was very jealous, and as soon as she had moved into the palace, she came to the kitchen and said, "From now on I will cook for the prime minister."

I was surprised, but I could hardly argue with my employer's wife. So I just bowed and asked what I was to prepare for her and how I could help. She thanked me in a rather uncivil manner; I could see that my friend Osore, the valet, gave her assistance, though later he explained to me that he couldn't refuse to help Obote's wife. I replied quite coldly that it was none of my business. But of course I felt hurt. I had always treated Osore like a brother; he was one of my two good friends.

The next day Miria came into the kitchen, put on an apron, and stood by the stove. I politely carried out all her requests, handing her ladles, spoons, and knives. What did she cook? I can't remember. But I do remember that the waiters took it to the table and served it to the prime minister, and he began to chew, one spoonful, then a second, until at last he asked, "Who made this?"

"I did," said Miria.

"What is this?" shouted Obote. "What the hell does this mean? We have a chef to do this!"

"A wife should cook for her husband. The chef can cook for other people," said Miria, taken aback.

Obote gave her a withering look. "The cooking is Otonde's job," he said angrily. "And yours is to eat what he prepares."

And he had them serve what I had cooked. Because of course I was no fool, and in the meantime I had managed to make soup and a meat dish as well.

Miria was deeply offended, though of course she couldn't say that. So she smiled, but she never forgot about it. From then on I had a sworn enemy in her, and more than once after that I had problems because of her.

I was always sweet and polite to her, and she was to me too. She was as sweet and polite to me as you can only be toward someone you hate.

14.

Obote's terms in office were far from idyllic for the country. The army mutinied because their pay was too low, conflict arose between the president and the government, and the prime minister's political enemies were thrown in jail. On top of that, Obote was suspected—together with General Idi Amin—of making money by smuggling gold from war-torn Congo. When parliament tried to launch an inquiry into the matter, the two of them instantly staged a high-speed coup d'état. It was Obote who had the idea, and Amin who carried it out, leading the storm of the kabaka's palace himself.

Like the British, Obote regarded Amin as a useful idiot. He was sure he could control Amin's strength and brutality and exploit them for his own purposes.

The kabaka fled to London. Parliament was dissolved. Obote became the new president and put the leaders of the opposition—

including the opposition within his own party, the Uganda People's Congress—in jail, thus ending the young country's brief adventure with democracy.

By the will of God, after the coup I became chef to the president.

I never gave much thought to whether what he was doing was legal or not. Obote was my boss, he was from my tribe, he was like a brother to me. I could only be pleased that we were doing so well.

My work changed, drastically. As Prime Minister Obote's chef, I had cooked mainly for him and for the other employees. There were three of us in the kitchen, sometimes four, and that was enough.

As President Obote's chef, I had to cook for foreign delegations, and for all the employees in his administration, and that was several dozen people. I had to give instructions to at least ten other people in the kitchen and organize their work.

I started by dividing the kitchen into three departments: the Meat Department, the Vegetable Department, and the Cake and Dessert Department, which was also responsible for baking bread. Every day we baked Indian bread for breakfast and European-style bread for supper. I was always the first up, and in the kitchen by 5:00 a.m. I oversaw the work of every other cook, and I personally prepared all the dishes that went to the president's table. I tested the dough for the chapatis, I made pancakes, and when necessary I went to the bazaar for any missing items.

Odera Osore's work changed too, because he was promoted from valet to majordomo, in charge of all the valets.

Though he would never have admitted it, I know that he owed this promotion to his good relationship with Miria, Obote's wife. It was she who urged her husband to promote him, and she went on insisting until finally he lost patience and agreed to it.

Osore stopped coming out for a beer with me and Okuku, the chauffeur. He was always trying to suck up to Miria in every way he could. He helped her to choose the curtains; he went to the stores with her to buy bedding and clothes. Because Miria didn't like me, he preferred to keep us at a safe distance. I won't say that Okuku and I were sorry. But each of us runs his life as he thinks best for him. Osore chose the path of a toady, and there was nothing we could do about it.

What did Obote eat? Not much meat, but he adored *malakwang*, for example, a spicy vegetable, with sesame, pomegranate paste, ground nuts, and boiled vegetables. He also liked fish and usually had tilapia with vegetables on the side. And cassava—flour made from manioc tubers. Or *ugali*, which is cornmeal boiled in milk, with a fish fillet.

But most often he asked for British dishes. As I've said, he took me on because I knew how to cook for whites.

Everyone called the president "Doctor" because he had a doctorate. And Obote used to laugh and say that I was the doctor, not Obote. A stomach doctor.

My position in the palace rose, because the president couldn't imagine his kitchen without me. He felt that without me the other chefs would have smashed the kitchen to pieces. I introduced discipline: they didn't have to like me; they just had to fear me.

Of course, although I had a lot of new duties, it never occurred to Obote to give me a raise. I was still working for 390
shillings, as in the days when I'd been a junior chef starting
out. I had to earn extra money by baking cakes after hours for
rich people's parties.

The more Obote liked me, the more enemies I had. But they
couldn't do me any harm. Nobody could. Listen to this story,
for instance: One day I quarreled about something with the
president's brother Livingstone. Normally, we got on very well,
but that day there was something bothering him, and he was
extremely nasty to me. He started shouting at me, but I gave
as good as I got. Whoever's brother he was, he had no right to
shout at me.

Then I started to pummel him with my fists.

"Now you've gone too far," he said, and ran to Obote to
complain. I ran after him, to give him a kick as well.

We burst into the president's private office, his brother
first, then me. Sweating and agitated, I was still holding him
by the shirtsleeve.

"Milton, your chef is hitting me!" cried the brother.

Obote slowly looked up from his newspaper. He gazed at
me, then at his brother. Finally, he said through clenched
teeth, "Livingstone, haven't you got a home of your own?"

"Yes, I have," replied his brother in confusion.

"If you don't like it here, the door is open," said the president, and turned his back on us.

What had I done? And what did I have to do? I finished
hitting the brother and went back to the kitchen to get lunch
ready on time.

I was with Obote for many years. We knew each other very well, and I think he really liked me. While I was there, he got married, and his children were born, four sons.

But I arrived there penniless, and I remained penniless the whole time. Throughout Obote's administration I worked very hard, but by the end I had nothing: no savings, no car, not even a motorbike. Nothing.

Everything was about to change because of Idi Amin. For the better, and for the worse.

15.

Several years after their joint coup, relations between Obote and Amin were very tense. The president suspected the general of having organized at least one attempt on his life; the bullet brushed past his face, and the grenade thrown at him did not explode.

But he still thought Amin was too stupid to threaten his authority. He regarded him with superior indifference. In January 1971 he headed off to a Commonwealth summit in Singapore, having already decided that as soon as he returned, he'd put Amin in jail.

Except that Amin wasn't going to give him the opportunity. A few days after Obote's departure, the tanks rolled out onto the streets of Kampala. Soldiers blocked the main streets of Entebbe and Kampala. The putsch went smoothly, like a shell through the barrel of a tank. People had had enough of Obote, who had raised taxes and told them to tighten their belts. They regarded Amin's seizure of power as a gift from God.

If I were a bird
If I had wings
I would fly far away
To where Obote is hiding
And I'd bring him here for Amin.

That was the song sung that day by the soldiers and the common people of Uganda, who threw flowers in front of the tanks.

16.

In the kitchen, Otonde is very precise. When he's cooking there's no room for jokes or a single superfluous word. When his daughter-in-law and granddaughters start to laugh at something, he instantly casts them a look of reproach. In the kitchen there must be silence, order, and calm.

"In my kitchen it was always like that," he says. "Work is no joking matter. In the kitchen, I was the dictator."

And Otonde apologizes but says that even I must keep quiet and wait with my questions. Cooking is too serious a matter for him to be distracted.

So I watch in silence as his daughter-in-law and granddaughters cut up the vegetables. I watch as Otonde deftly skins and fillets the fish, as he removes the bones and prepares it for frying. I watch as he adds a solid dose of salt to it all.

"I add as much salt as for Amin," he says, and I don't know if I'm going to be able to swallow a mouthful of it, because Amin liked his food salted to excess.

Finally, I watch as over the pots Odera changes into a completely different person. A different kind of energy enters him from the kind I've seen in him earlier. I feel as if I'm witnessing a voodoo ritual. Otonde's face has changed; he moves differently; he looks younger and fitter, and he stands straighter.

But no, it's not voodoo. It's just a man who's in his right place, doing what he loves best.

The chicken is roasting, and we're just about to take the fish out of the frying pan. We go back to Idi Amin, who deposed his political patron, Milton Obote.

We heard the first shots in the presidential palace that afternoon. Nobody knew what was going on, though there had been signs for several days that something strange might happen. Ever since Obote had left for Singapore, the radio had stopped talking about him; instead, it talked mainly about Idi Amin. But for there to be a putsch? It would never have entered my mind. In Africa there had been more than twenty military coups before then, and many of the presidents I had cooked for on various occasions had ceased to be presidents. But I always thought Obote was in control of the situation.

Until suddenly they started shooting. Several people tried to escape from the palace, and my first reaction was to run away too. But I had no chance of escaping with my wife and small child.

Rumors reached us that the soldiers who had taken control of the city were murdering the Lango and the Luo. We were afraid, but trying to run away was pointless. We locked ourselves inside the palace and waited. For what? For death. We thought the Kakwa—Amin's tribe, the one that was going to be in power now—were going to fire at us.

Luckily, nobody had the courage to enter the palace without Amin's knowledge. The soldiers merely surrounded us. And waited.

Finally, toward evening, General Idi Amin arrived in person, in a jeep, with a pistol on either side of him. He ran into the palace. He called everyone together. He ordered us to come down into the vestibule.

We were sure they were going to shoot us then and there. Some were even trying to hide behind others.

But Amin said, "Don't be afraid. For you nothing is going to change. Go on working just as you always have."

And he gave orders to be served supper.

Did I have it ready? Of course I did. The previous coup had taught me that generals are there for coups. But a cook is there to have clean hands and a clean apron. And to cook. Nothing excuses you from your work, because once they've carried out their putsch, they'll arrive with empty bellies, and as long as you have something good for them to eat, there's a chance they won't kill you.

Can you imagine what would have happened if Amin had spent all day carrying out his coup, arrived at the palace in the evening, and found there was no supper waiting for him? He'd have given us hell. Out of hunger. People go mad from hunger; I've seen it many times.

I had cooked tilapia and goat pilaf; I remembered that Amin liked it. We served it all on a fresh tablecloth, with silver service, left over from the British. Amin must have felt that he had won the coup and now he deserved a tasty meal. Tell me, what could be a better reward than excellent food served by a well-dressed cook in a good suit and shoes?

Just as when they overthrew the kabaka, the soldiers pitched camp in the garden around the palace. We had chicken and pilaf ready for them as well. They had had a tough day too.

17.

Almost as soon as Amin had finished supper, he ran off somewhere. And there was very sad news in store for me.

The soldiers from the nearby barracks called to say they had a corpse, and that it was someone from our staff, because he'd been driving a car that belonged to the palace.

No one wanted to go and fetch the body; they were all afraid. Now that we knew it was safe inside the palace, we thought it better not to stick our noses outside. But someone had to go. So I went, especially because I already sensed the worst.

The soldiers led me into a yard where there were at least ten cars. In one of them, a pickup truck, was a body with about fifteen bullet holes in it.

It was Solomon Okuku, President Obote's chauffeur. My best friend.

They helped me to carry his body to my car. I drove it to the palace and put it in one of the cold stores. I couldn't restrain my sobbing. There, outside the cold store, I sat until morning. I cried and screamed like a little child.

It was only later that I found out Okuku had died a hero. When he saw Kakwa soldiers from Amin's tribe murdering Lango and Luo, he took a truck, drove to the suburbs of Kampala where the people from his village lived, loaded the vehicle as full as possible, and drove to Entebbe, from where the boats sailed to Kenya. He managed to drive there, because the soldiers were still poorly organized. But on his way back they stopped him at one of their checkpoints. The soldiers said he had been the first to take out a weapon and start shooting. Apparently, he killed one of them, and then they killed him. But I don't believe it. Okuku was a very gentle person.

A few days later, when the situation was a bit calmer, I organized transport to Kenya for Okuku's body. I asked Odero Osore, the valet and our mutual friend, if he would help. Osore said he'd like to but he had a lot to do now. Amin was large and burly, so he had to buy him new clothes—everything from shoes to shirts and suits. "But, brother," said Osore, "I am sure you will manage."

Okuku's body sailed across the lake to Kisumu, where his family came to collect it. He had a fine funeral, attended by a very large number of people, including the ones he had driven to the ferry and who, thanks to him, had survived.

At the time I had to blink back my tears and go on working as usual. Under Amin it wasn't the same as under Obote, who loved me and under whom I could take a lot of liberties. Here—as I knew from the start—my life depended on my cooking skills.

18.

Although Amin's men had killed Okuku, I believed that Amin would be a good president. Especially because my life improved a lot.

It started like this: a year and a half before Amin's coup,

the kabaka died in Great Britain. People said Obote had poisoned him, but I don't know.

The kabaka was still very popular in Uganda. And once Amin was president, he had his remains flown back to Kampala and held a grand funeral for him. Amin stood in the front row, by the coffin, and wept as if his own father were lying in it and as if he hadn't helped Obote to depose the kabaka.

The kabaka's body was brought from England by two officers. They stayed at the palace, and as soon as they arrived, I made them supper: vegetable soup, steak and kidney pie—which I had learned to make at the memsahib's—and chocolate pudding.

In the morning the British officers had a meeting with Amin and immediately started asking him questions about the supper.

"Mr. President, it was delicious. Do you have a white chef?"

"He is just as white as I am," Amin said with a laugh. And when they refused to believe it, he summoned me. I couldn't understand a word of what they were saying, but I bowed politely and kept repeating, "Thank you, thank you."

The British officers were full of admiration, and Amin was puffed up with pride. He was keen to prove to the whites that blacks are not inferior to them. So as soon as the British officers had flown back to London, he sent for me.

"How much do you earn, Otonde?" he asked.

"Three hundred and ninety shillings, Mr. President," I replied.

"Really? So little?" he cried in astonishment. And at once he called for his chief of administration.

"Call the Lake Victoria Hotel and ask how much their head chef earns. And then raise Otonde's salary to the same amount. *Immediately!*" he stressed.

The chief of administration nodded and, though unwillingly, made the call.

It turned out that the head chef there earned 1,017 shillings.

From then on I started earning that much too. What's more, the president gave orders for me to receive three months' back pay at that rate, to cover the whole period since he had come to power.

At that point I earned more than any other member of the administration at the presidential palace. The chief of administration, whose salary hadn't been changed since Obote's time either, had to swallow this bitter pill.

And soon after that he had to swallow another. One day he summoned me to the vestibule.

"Otonde, I have a surprise for you," he said, forcing himself to smile. I wiped my hands on my apron and followed him. In the driveway stood a brand-new, shiny black Mercedes-Benz.

"It's a gift from the president. So you'll have something to go shopping in," he said. I bowed and said thank you for the wonderful gift and promised I would continue to work hard to try to please the president.

He had nothing to say in reply. He didn't have a car at his disposal, though he too worked hard and with dedication. Many of the other employees had no car either. My God! I feel ashamed of it now, but at the time I felt very proud of myself as I thumbed my nose at them all. Of course I suffered when I saw how Amin and his people treated Obote's people. Many of my acquaintances had had to flee the country, and several, including Okuku the chauffeur, had been killed. But for me Amin's government meant a triple raise and a shiny Mercedes. I'd be lying if I said I didn't like that.

19.

The flight control tower at London's Heathrow Airport had quite a problem. A plane approaching from the south was asking for permission to land, declaring that the president of Uganda was on board, Field Marshal Idi Amin.

As Major Iain Grahame, Amin's former superior officer in the King's African Rifles, remembers the incident, "Nobody in this country had the faintest idea why he had come here. The queen was fortunately in residence and she was prevailed upon to give him lunch the following day. After lunch the queen looked up over her coffee cup to her guest and said, 'Would you please tell me, Mr. President, to what do we owe the unexpected honor of your visit to Britain?' And Amin burst out laughing and then he said, 'In Uganda, Your Majesty, it is very difficult to buy a pair of size fourteen brown shoes.'"

Amin's love of all things British was legendary. To his annually increasing list of titles—the formula "His Excellency, President for Life, Field Marshal, Lord of All the Beasts of the Earth and Fishes of the Seas, VC, DSO, MC" was recited on the radio every time Amin's name was mentioned—he added "Last King of Scotland and Conqueror of the British Empire." He ordered a military band to be formed, which—dressed in kilts—was to grace all major ceremonies by playing the bagpipes.

"I am responsible for his love of Scotland," says Major Grahame. "Because I am a Scot. On many occasions I shared a tent with him and we talked into the night. I would talk to him about tribalism and about the Scottish clans."

In fact Amin hadn't flown to London to buy shoes. He'd come to buy weapons to reinforce the Ugandan army and be able to hold his neighbors in check, including Tanzania, where Milton Obote was in hiding. When the arms purchases failed, he was furious and declared Britain one of his greatest enemies.

Anyone who saw Amin as a jovial simpleton who could easily be controlled must have known after a few months of his rule how very much they had been mistaken.

20.

The new president demanded just one thing of me. Because he was a Muslim, he insisted that everyone who prepared food for him be circumcised. If I wanted to go on working at the palace, I would have to have my foreskin cut off.

I was quite surprised, because I didn't think religion seemed that important to Amin. But his decision was un-equivocal. The chief of administration, Oyite Ojok, had himself circumcised. So did I, as the head chef, and so did my friend Odero Osore, who had become Amin's majordomo. After Okuku's death, Osore and I became close friends again, which pleased me. We sometimes used to meet after work. He was the only person I could confide in; I could tell him how much I missed Okuku, and he was the only one who under-stood.

Once we had done it, everyone else was circumcised too—the cooks, waiters, and assistants. We were all given appointments at Mulago Hospital, which took care of the president and his family. The procedure took less than a minute. I could go on working for Amin without any problem.

Islam only took on greater significance for Amin when he broke off relations with Europe and Israel and became friends with Colonel Gaddafi. Gaddafi even built a mosque in downtown Kampala, where the president sometimes used to go to pray. I met Gaddafi twice. He hugged me like a brother and ate my food, but I never had the opportunity to talk to him at length.

When it was plain to see that Amin had ever greater respect for the Muslims, something strange happened to Osore. He suddenly decided to adopt Islam. It made everyone laugh, because he was obviously doing it purely to gain Amin's affection, just as he had once done everything to make Obote's wife, Miria, like him. Even Amin thought it was funny. He started calling Osore "El Haj"; only people who have made the pilgrimage to Mecca and Medina are addressed that way, but Osore hadn't been to those places yet.

At the time I thought Osore was going too far. We didn't have to toady to Amin. He was generous anyway; even for agreeing to have myself circumcised, I received a gift from him. But I didn't pass comment on Osore's choices. We still used to meet after work, and we still talked about the things that mattered most to us.

We were both happy with our work. Obote had never once said "thank you" for making him a meal, nor had he ever thanked Osore for getting his clothes ready. He looked down on everyone, even his own family. But Amin? If I made something special, he gave me an envelope full of extra money and thanked me for the food five times over.

21.

In Amin's day I had the best clothes and a Mercedes for work, and in time I bought myself a private car, too, a Volkswagen Beetle. My wife gave birth to a second child. My son Edward went to a very good school, attended by the children of politicians and officials. Meanwhile, Amin very often urged me, "Otonde, you're such a talented cook; you earn a good salary. You should have more women."

One evening, he saw me talking to a young woman at supper. He came up to us, threw his arms around our shoulders, and started questioning the girl, asking what she thought of me and if she wanted to get to know me better. He said I was a superb cook and that by my side she'd be sure to have plenty of good food.

There were women who came to parties at the palace especially to find a husband or a lover. One of the ministers, perhaps? Or maybe an influential official? And if not one of those, a chef was good too. In a country where there was a lack of food, he might even be better.

What was that girl to say when the president asked her in person if she wanted to get to know me better? She soon became my second wife. I wasn't a Muslim, but we Luo can have several wives too.

Amin was obsessed with women. He was always having affairs, he had lots of lovers, he was always hanging around women. It was impossible to refuse him; if a woman rejected him, she had to flee the country, or else Amin would take revenge. On occasion, if he wanted to conquer a married woman, his bodyguards killed her husband.

He also transferred this obsession to others. After my second marriage, he often repeated that two wives was too few for me. If we went somewhere, if there was a party, and I started talking to a girl, one of Amin's men, whose name was Saba Saba, would appear. He always had a briefcase full of cash with him, and he'd discreetly take me aside and say, "The president wants you to have fun with the lady."

And he'd give me several thousand shillings.

It wasn't exactly an order, and not exactly a joke, but Amin wasn't to be refused. It was a sort of show for him. He sat and watched; he enjoyed watching other people getting intimate.

As a result, thanks to Amin I had two more Ugandan wives. I brought one of them back from a trip to Jinja with Amin, and the other was from the same district as his family village. Before the wedding the president always handed us an envelope full of money and assured us he'd take care of us and our children. And he really did remember us; I cannot accuse him of neglecting us. We would receive extra cash, and we never went short of food or clothing.

I reached my peak as a chef under Amin too. The kitchen's annual budget totaled eight million shillings, and I was entirely responsible for it. If we had a reception, I was able to prepare more than one hundred roast chickens by myself. I didn't find it at all tiring. I loved my job.

My great invention was whole roasted goat. We'd remove its innards, cut off its beard, stuff it with rice, potatoes, carrots, parsley, peas, and some herbs and spices—naturally, all mixed with goat meat cut into small pieces. We'd roast it in the oven and color it a bit, and as a finishing touch we'd stick its beard back on. It would be brought to the table in a standing position, as if it were alive. Everyone was surprised to see a goat looking as if it had come straight from the pasture but which was ready to eat in minutes.

My first few years with Amin were golden times. I have two smart suits left from those days.

And that's all.

22.

Amin was afraid of everyone who might pose a threat to his power—most of all, people who were well educated, were rich, or had connections with the previous government. So the police and the army were given an unlimited mandate: within the majesty of the law they could kill people. The Public Safety Unit murdered with impunity and without limitations.

Their lockups were right in the center of Kampala. People on their way to work often heard the screams of prisoners being tortured, or gunshots, though Amin's men usually killed their victims with hammers or machetes.

According to Henry Kyemba, a former minister in Amin's government, several years after the coup people were being killed by the hundreds. Instead of burying the corpses, the security services dumped them in the Nile, where they were eaten by crocodiles. Afraid for his life, Kyemba fled to England.

Every year it grew worse. Everyone in the palace knew someone who had lost his life. People we knew personally— ministers from Obote's time, UPC politicians—disappeared without a trace. And later they'd be found—dead, with their hands, feet, ears, and tongues cut off . . .

You ask how I could cook for such a monster. Well, I had four wives and five children. Amin had tied me to him so that I couldn't leave. I didn't even notice it happening. I couldn't have coped without his money. I was entirely dependent on him, and he knew that. He made his bodyguards, ministers, and even his friends similarly dependent on him.

I also knew that there was no way I could help the people he killed—how on earth? By poisoning Amin? I'd have lost my life too, and how could I be sure the next president wouldn't do more killing?

We palace staff knew we were working for a madman who might get up in the morning and have us killed. But for a long time everything was all right at the palace. Until the pilaf incident.

It was like this. One time I made a very sweet pilaf with raisins. It's a simple dish: you boil rice, add raisins, and a sprinkling of cinnamon. Moses Amin, Amin's thirteen-year-old son, who had inherited his father's appetite, wolfed down so much of it that he almost exploded. He started having a terrible stomachache.

Amin decided his son had been poisoned. He went running about the palace, screaming, "If something happens to him, I'll kill you all!"

I didn't wait to see what was coming next. I took the child, sneaked him out the back door, and drove him to Mulago Hospital. We went to see the doctor who took care of the president's family, who started pressing the boy's belly. Meanwhile, I asked the telephone operator to put me through to the palace. Amin was going out of his mind, shouting, "Poison! Poison!"

Everyone was convinced I really had poisoned Moses Amin and then run away, and they were all going to die because of me. So when the chief of administration heard my voice, he immediately handed the receiver to the president. Later I found out that Amin had been holding the phone in his left hand while putting a pistol to the head of one of the cooks with his right.

Meanwhile, the doctor was still pressing the boy's belly, until finally the boy let out a tremendous fart.

"I feel much better," he said.

The doctor reported to Amin that there was nothing wrong with his son; he'd simply eaten too much and would be breaking wind for a while longer. For many weeks afterward Amin thought it an excellent joke. Every time he saw me, he'd start to laugh and merrily clap me on the shoulder, exclaiming, "A fart, a fart!"

I didn't find it quite so amusing. If I hadn't kept my cool and taken Moses to the hospital, I could have lost my life.

23.

To this day, people in Kampala tell how Amin drank the blood of those he had killed. Or that he ate pieces of their livers. Apparently, this is what he did to Charles Arube, for instance, his chief of staff who tried to depose him. "On several occasions when I was Minister of Health, Amin insisted on being left alone with his victims' bodies . . . There is of course no evidence for what he does in private," writes Henry Kyemba. "It is universally believed in Uganda that he engages in blood rituals."*

But elsewhere Kyemba admits that Amin did all sorts of things to make people think he was unpredictable. Maybe that's what happened that time too?

"Of course Amin had people killed," says Major Grahame unambiguously. "I was angry, and sad about it. But I cannot believe he wanted to eat them."

Amin was shocking, and people were afraid of him—which meant they let him get away with more than they would otherwise. This strategy suited the European countries too: by referring to the example of Amin, cannibal and savage, they could pooh-pooh African independence.

There are no witnesses who saw Amin eating human flesh. Even Kyemba, who wrote his memoirs shortly after Amin tried to kill him, does not establish whether he was a cannibal. There's nothing but secondhand stories and rumors.

But I'm at the very source, aren't I? Who better to ask about Amin's cannibalism than Otonde Odera, his longtime chef?

---

* Henry Kyemba, *A State of Blood: The Inside Story of Idi Amin's Reign of Fear* (Ace Books, 1977), 108–9.

After spending a week talking to him, I finally pluck up the courage. "Lots of people say that Amin was a cannibal . . . ," I say.

Odera takes a deep breath. He's clearly been expecting the question. He sits on a box under the large tree where we've been filling the hours with our conversations and thinks for a while. Finally, he speaks.

"I swear to God I never saw such a thing. Of course I've heard people talking about it. I've very often been asked if I ever cooked human flesh for him.

"But no. It never happened.

"I never saw any meat of unfamiliar origin, or that I hadn't bought myself, in the fridges and cold stores under my charge. There was never a single occasion when the soldiers brought meat whose origin I didn't know. I was the only one who did the shopping."

And then Otonde starts to cry.

The tears drip off his chin and onto his checked shirt. He's staring at me, as if wanting to make sure I believe him. As if he can't conceive of having to answer that sort of question. As if he weren't capable of imagining that the man who tripled his salary—the man thanks to whom he had four wives and two suits, who gave him envelopes full of cash for his children's keep and schooling, the man for whom every day he made nutritious pilafs, baked fish, and chopped vegetables with his own hands, whom he fed as a mother feeds her child, and whose good mood and well-being he looked after for many years—that this man could have eaten the livers of other human beings.

24.

Amin was given the nickname Dada because, when caught with one of his lovers, he explained himself by saying, "She's not my lover, she's my *dada*." In Swahili *dada* means "sister." It made his army colleagues laugh so much they started to call him that, and it stuck.

He had five official wives. They didn't live at the palace, but had their own house right next to it. They only came in for meals, and then they left. If they talked to me, it was usually to ask about the desserts—fruitcake or cheesecake. Occasionally, they came to the kitchen in the evening for a snack. Amin was very rarely at the palace, so I think they were lonely. And we all know there's nothing to cheer you up like something sweet.

Did I talk to them? No. It's not the chef's job to talk to the president's wives, so even if they tried, I always politely but firmly ended the conversation. Amin had his eyes and ears everywhere, and I could be sure one of the cooks was bound to report to the services. That was all I needed, for someone to start gabbing that I was fraternizing with the president's wives.

They didn't have an easy life in any case.

One time Amin drove beyond the city on his own. He very often went out alone, without his bodyguards, but that night there was a phone call to say he had had an accident. We were horrified. One of his wives, Madina, started getting dressed to go to the hospital. We were all in a sort of frenzy.

As we were running around pointlessly, suddenly Amin appeared. One of his hands was bandaged, but there was nothing seriously wrong with him. And yet he was furious. He saw Madina, beautifully dressed, and right there in the doorway he started to hit her. "Are you dressed like that because you thought I was dead?" he shouted.

And he went on hitting her, wildly out of control.

We were all stunned. Nobody dared lift a finger; we were afraid Amin would kill Madina before our eyes and then start on us. Until a man named Kizito, whom Amin trusted greatly, cried, "Mr. President, please stop!"

Instantly, Amin took his pistol from its holster and fired at Kizito. Once, twice, three times. All the bullets missed, and although Kizito was standing very nearby, he survived. So did Madina.

None of the staff said a single word. We all went back to our duties. But we knew that if in our presence Amin could beat his wife, and if he could shoot at Kizito, whom he trusted like a brother, he could shoot any of us at any moment.

Each of us had to find our own way of dealing with it. Oyok, the chief of administration, had become meek and was always trying to second-guess Amin's wishes before he expressed them. Osore, the majordomo, my friend, had become a devout Muslim; he prayed with his face turned toward Mecca every day before work and in between tasks, and whenever he could, he went to the mosque. What about me? I believed I cooked well enough for Amin not to kill me. But with each passing day in the palace my faith in getting out alive dwindled.

Two of Amin's five wives died in tragic circumstances, probably killed on his orders. Especially tragic was the fate of Kay; Amin not only had her killed but also chopped to pieces.

And then the time came for me too.

25.

I came back early one morning from Kenya, where I had been visiting my mother. Through a small bathroom window I saw soldiers surrounding our house. Several were lying on the ground; others were creeping up. I didn't know what it was about, but it looked really serious.

Finally, someone knocked at the door. It was a Ugandan army officer. I had never seen him before. When I opened the door, he pushed me so hard that I almost fell over. He ordered me to show him what I had in my suitcase.

All it contained was a shirt and a pair of pants.

He searched it carefully, and when he found nothing but clothing, he said, "Never mind that there's nothing here. We know you wanted to kill the president. Luckily, someone reported it to us."

Did I want to kill Amin? No. I was young, I wanted to live, I didn't want to kill anyone. I started to weep as I tried to explain that it wasn't true. Elizabeth threw herself at the officer's feet. But nobody would listen to me or to her. The soldiers laid a metal bar on my shoulders, tied me to it, and grabbed me by the elbows. They threw me in the bed of a truck, drove to a dungeon on Lake Victoria, and pushed me in with the other prisoners. That was a dreadful place. Someone was groaning. Someone else was weeping. There were several men lying on the floor; I don't know if they were dying or already dead.

I knew no one ever came back from those places. Everyone who lived in Amin's Uganda knew that.

Suddenly, from a world where you encounter the president, ministers, and beautifully dressed people every day, you end up in a dungeon where the walls are covered in blood and where people are awaiting death. I wept in terror.

When it started to get through to me that it wasn't a dream, but that I too was awaiting death with them, I started to pray. I don't know why, because I had never prayed before. But right then I said, "O God, I know everyone dies. I know my turn is coming too. But I beg you, not here, not now. I desperately want to live a bit longer. O God, You didn't save me as the only one of fourteen siblings just for me to perish here. You didn't protect me from the hyenas and the hippo for my life to end this way."

I didn't sleep at all that night. The next day at dawn some soldiers appeared. They led me out. I was sure I was going to my death, but they didn't kill me. Instead, they pushed me into a car and drove me to the presidential palace, where Elizabeth and the children were waiting for me.

My Ugandan wives had run off as soon as I was arrested. I never saw them again.

They packed us all into a vehicle. We had no idea where they were taking us. Elizabeth was crying, but softly. And I was wondering what mistake I had made. Maybe I'd been too rough? Maybe people regarded me as unpleasant? But I hadn't done anyone enough harm for them to send me to my death! Anyone who'd gone to Amin and told him I was planning to poison him knew perfectly well that for that I would be killed, and so would my wives and all my children.

We passed the city of Jinja, where the Nile flows out of the lake. "Aha," I thought, "they're taking us to Maga Maga." That was an execution site.

But they didn't turn off to Maga Maga.

Only when we arrived in Busia, a town on the Kenyan border, did I realize they weren't going to kill us. God had decided to spare me. For what reason I still don't know. Idi Amin had granted me my life.

The soldiers got hold of a Kenyan officer and told him I was the cook from the presidential palace. They said I had no ID card with me, because I was being thrown out of their country with immediate effect. The Kenyans conferred for a while, then took off my handcuffs and told me to go home. I hadn't a single cooking pot, or even a change of pants. Nothing.

I had to start all over again from the beginning.

26.

After Odera's exile, Amin ruled the country for two more years, until he provoked a war with Tanzania. He was soon overthrown by the Tanzanian army.

In May 1980, Milton Obote returned to Kampala.

As soon as he returned, Obote sent one of his bodyguards to find me. This man spent several days looking for me in Nairobi. Finally, he succeeded.

Since Amin had thrown me out of Uganda, I had had lots of jobs. I was a *boda boda* motorbike driver, and I delivered paper napkins to the hotels. The bodyguard found me at a casino where I was helping to do the cleaning.

When I found out that Obote was the president again and

that he was looking for me, I immediately gave up my job and went with the bodyguard to Kampala. There they sat me down and told me to wait. A few minutes later I saw the president opening the door. He glanced at me and . . . immediately left the room. He didn't say a single word.

The bodyguards told me, "Sorry, Otonde, there has clearly been a mistake. It wasn't you but Odero Osore, the majordomo, they were looking for. Miria liked him very much; evidently, she had asked for him to be found, and because you have similar family names, by accident they brought you."

I thought my heart would fall to pieces. What was I to do? I didn't even have the money for a ticket back to Kenya.

Suddenly one of the waiters brought me a cold bottle of cola. He opened it and poured it into a glass.

I couldn't understand a thing. Why suddenly the cola?

Soon after that, Obote's assistant appeared and said that the president had given instructions for them to take me to the Lake Victoria Hotel, where there was a room for me.

Now I was totally confused. Cola? A room at a five-star hotel? Then why had Obote left the room at the sight of me?

It turned out that as soon as he saw me, he had burst into tears. I was told later that he cried like a baby. He didn't want anyone else to see him crying. I went back to the palace and continued working for him.

And later it turned out that Miria really was looking for Odero Osore. But Osore—the only member of the administration to have converted to Islam—had gone with Amin to Saudi Arabia, where he went on working for him as his majordomo there.

27.

Milton Obote ruled Uganda for the next five years. Fortune granted him a unique opportunity: very few deposed leaders return to their post. And he blew it.* When a rebellion against him erupted in the north of the country, he responded with a brutal attack that—though it was meant to be aimed at the rebels—largely affected civilians. Once again, as in Amin's day, the army tortured and killed people. Yet these crimes were commissioned not by a burly ex-boxer regarded as a half-wit but by a well-mannered, well-read gentleman, so they were less spectacular, and the Western media weren't so eager to write about them. Although Obote's second term of office cost several hundreds of thousands of people their lives, almost nothing has been said about it.

In 1985, insurgents captured Kampala under the leadership of Yoweri Museveni, who is still president of Uganda to this day. Milton Obote had to flee the country for a second time.

When the guerrillas came, once again I had everything ready to serve. But this time it wasn't like with Obote and Amin. The guerrillas had brought their own cooks, whom they trusted and who had cooked for them during their fight. They wouldn't eat anything cooked by me. To them I was suspect.

I never exchanged a single word with the new president; we just passed each other in the corridor. I doubt he knew who I was. New times had come. A few days later I was ordered to leave the palace. So with my wife and children I went back to

---

* Julian Marshall, obituary of Milton Obote, *Guardian*, October 12, 2005.

Kenya. I only had two suits, a few suitcases, and a motorbike. Once more I had to start again from nothing.

I found a job as a driver for a bishop from the Power of Jesus Around the World Church. Thanks to him, I found Jesus. I started going to church. To this day I go there every Sunday, I stand in the front row, and through my unusual life—my life as Jonah, who managed to escape from the belly of the whale—I bear witness to the greatness of the Lord and to the extraordinary paths He leads us on. I know that not long from now I shall meet Jesus, just as I see you here before me.

I am ready.

I am over eighty now and have less and less strength. My house—well, you can see for yourself. The holes in the walls and in the roof are so large that you can put your hand through them. When it rains, it rains on our heads. When the wind blows, it blows in our faces. You've also seen our outhouse—a deep hole in the ground. Whenever I go to relieve myself at night, I'm afraid I'll fall in there and drown in shit before anyone notices. Would you have guessed that the man who cooked for presidents lives like that? Whose hand was shaken by Colonel Gaddafi and the emperor Haile Selassie?

And although my strength is waning, I have to do more and more at home on my own. My Elizabeth is still with me, but she's very feeble now. I mean, she's all right physically, but her head can't keep up with her body. Sometimes she leaves the house and can't find her way back. Lately there have been moments when she looks at me, smiles, and asks me who I am.

28.

I returned to my village, and several years later Odero Osore came back too. He had served Idi Amin as his majordomo to the day he died. Despite various misunderstandings, we were good friends; we'd known each other for many years. So as soon as someone from my village was going to his vicinity—he lived half an hour away—I asked them to give him my best wishes.

For some reason he never reciprocated. He never responded through anyone, not so much as "God be with you."

For a while I thought maybe it was because I believed in Jesus, while he was a Muslim. But why should that obstruct our friendship? I have many friends who are Muslims. I couldn't understand it.

Until one day I met a man at the market in Kisumu who used to work at the presidential palace as an errand boy. I told him about the knotty problem I had with Osore. I said I'd like to go and see him, to ask if he bore a grudge against me, and if he remembered the old days.

This man stared at me as if I were a fool.

"Otonde," he said, "don't you know anything?"

"What the hell should I know?" I said in surprise.

"Otonde, it was Osore who told Amin you wanted to kill him. It was because of him that you were within an inch of being killed."

It turned out everyone in the palace knew that. Everyone except me.

29.

Osore died a few years ago. We never met again, so I couldn't tell him face-to-face that I knew he had betrayed me.

Nor could I tell him that thanks to Christ I had forgiven him. I said in front of the entire congregation, "Lord Jesus, please save the soul of my brother Osore."

To finish, my brother, let us pray. Let us pray for you and for your loved ones. Let us pray for my wife. For my children. For the souls of Solomon Okuku and Odero Osore.

Let us pray for the souls of Milton Obote and Idi Amin.

O God, remember them all.

O God, remember me too, whom You have cherished so dearly. One thing I know—although I have less and less strength, although blood occasionally flows from my ear at night, although sometimes I feel like Job, who lost everything, O Lord, I know that You are beside me at all times. And I know that You did not save me just for me to die in this way, beside a wife who no longer recognizes me, in a house through which the wind howls, with an outhouse I'm afraid of falling into. O God, deep in my heart I believe that You will reach out to me. I know there is still beauty in store for me. I know, because You did not give me this sort of a life for it to end in this place, in this way.

Even if I go to sleep hungry—and there are days like that—O God, You lay me in a hole in the ground like a baby. And just as my mother once did, You wrap me in a placenta.

Snack
អាហារសម្រន់

As Brother Pouk's cook, I was given my own home, almost at the center of K5, our base. At first I lived there on my own, with everything I needed for cooking: pots, spoons, knives, chopping boards. Only later, when the camp had grown, did another cook share the cabin with me.

Near our cabin stood another one, quite empty. I didn't know who or what it was for. Nobody talked about it, and I didn't ask. I'd learned by then that in the Organization if they didn't tell you something themselves, it was better not to ask.

Every day I got up just after five to have breakfast ready for Pol Pot. From my cabin I could see his, so I often worked outside; I wanted to hear him getting up, bathing, and getting dressed.

It gave me pleasure.

At first, as I cooked, the bodyguards used to come up, one or two of them, and watch my hands. Maybe they were afraid I would try to poison him? But then Pol Pot would say, "Leave our Moeun alone."

He trusted me entirely.

So the bodyguards left me in peace, though they went on watching me. But now they did it from a distance, discreetly.

And not out of fear for Pol Pot's life, but because I was young and very pretty, and they were young too.

At seven I took breakfast to Brother Pouk and the other leaders. Sister Khieu Thirith, who was Pol Pot's secretary, taught me how to bake the kind of bread they make in Europe. We had yeast and a special tin. I'd leaven the dough, leave it overnight, and put it in the oven in its tin the next morning. Everyone said it came out very well.

At the camp we had large gardens where we grew all the fruits and vegetables we needed. Brother Pouk stressed at every step that we must be self-sufficient. Every soldier had the right to come to the garden with his mess tin and pick whatever he felt like eating, then light a fire and cook it up for himself.

They'd already been living in the jungle for several years, so by the time I got there, the gardens covered several hundred square yards and produced a large variety of fruits and vegetables. Our boys hunted wild pigs, caught fish in the lake, and bought hens from the peasants. We had our own hens too, running loose among the huts, but there were never many of them, because they caused too much confusion. So we usually bought chickens, and the same went for rice. Most of the peasants loved us and never refused to help us.

People from the villages that were under our control worked in the gardens. They planted everything imaginable there, so every day I could think up something new to cook. The sisters from the villages taught me how to cook other things and how to use the plants we had in the gardens. There was water spinach growing there, a leguminous plant that can be eaten on its own; you just have to add a little garlic and

fish sauce. There were pumpkins, tomatoes, eggplants, and bitter gourds—that's a kind of squash, but with a warty skin—as
well as cabbages, wax gourds, broccoli, and onions.

I used to add bamboo shoots or banana flowers to the
soups and salads. Bananas grew everywhere. I also used to
make a banana flower salad that Brother Pouk liked very
much. We had tamarind, taro, luffas, and winged beans—the
pods have jagged edges, and you can eat the flowers, the
leaves, the pods, and even the roots, which taste a bit like
potato. As appetizers we also used to serve bamboo shoots
and fruit.

The common soldiers learned how to eat turtle eggs from
the Khmer Loeu, the highland Khmer. I learned to make soup
out of turtle meat, though Pol Pot wasn't fond of it. He preferred snake-meat soup.

Once in a while the Khmer Loeu would slaughter an elephant. This was always a great event, and they had special
songs for the occasion. We'd dry some of the meat and store it
for leaner times; it never went off, not even in the hottest
weather. But our leaders refused to eat elephant meat.

Brother Pouk wisely taught his soldiers that wherever they
went, first they should go and see the local gardeners, who
would give them seedlings, and then the soldiers should plant
them out in the jungle. In our country the earth bears fruit
easily, so whenever the soldiers went to a new site to pitch
camp, set an ambush, or scout out the terrain, they took water
spinach seedlings and squash, eggplant, or bitter melon seeds
with them in special bags. Or hot chili peppers, which they
loved, and thanks to which they had healthy stomachs. The
commanders also taught them that the seeds of some of the

plants they ate could be spat out and covered with earth, and then there was a chance of new plants growing from them. Brother Pouk used to say we should grow food at as many sites in the jungle as possible. Then the enemy would never be able to destroy us.

And it was true. Whenever we moved to a new location, we usually found some edible plants. Even in places where we stopped only for a short time, we'd find wild crops of chili peppers or squash; evidently, someone had spat out a seed and made sure it sprouted, in accordance with Brother Pouk's instructions.

Brother Pouk was always pleased to see these wild crops in the jungle. He knew Cambodia was under threat from the Vietnamese, the Thais, the Americans, and the French. And that the entire nation had to learn to be self-sufficient. If we wanted to survive as the Khmer, as the descendants of the people who built the ancient temples at Angkor Wat, we had to be capable of coping for ourselves in every way, from food to clothing and medical aid.

There were just two things we didn't have: salt, and medication for malaria.

The Khmer Loeu weren't familiar with salt, so in Ratanakiri there was nowhere to buy it. But it was possible to live without it. It was worse that there were no malaria drugs. Lots of people died of it, and most of them could have been saved if only we'd had the simplest medications. There was nothing we could do to stop fine warriors committed to the revolution from dying. Even Pol Pot fell sick with malaria, though he did have some medication.

Do you mean to say, brother, that if we were all equal, we should have been equal when it came to malaria too? Brother, in those days we were fighting against Lon Nol's troops, and there were American bombs falling on us. Pol Pot was the head of our movement. His survival was more important than any of our lives.

·◦❧ *Dinner* ❧◦·
Darkë

Sheqerpare

The Story of Mr. K.,
Enver Hoxha's Chef

1.

Every morning we had self-criticism sessions in a room near the kitchen.

Even if I thought I'd done everything right, I had to find fault with myself. You couldn't be satisfied with what you'd accomplished; that would have aroused suspicion. So I'd say I'd added a pinch too much seasoning or that Hoxha had had to wait half a minute too long for his dinner. Hoxha's time was valuable, so those half minutes were a serious violation.

The doctors, the waiters, and even the girl who arranged the flowers were all obliged to identify their mistakes. They were written down in special notebooks, and later, on an annual basis, we were appraised accordingly.

After a year in the job, I had to rack my brains to think up something new; I couldn't keep talking about seasoning or delays all the time. That's what self-criticism was for—to make you change and improve, not remain in place.

Did they trust me? No. They didn't trust anyone. Sulo Gradeci, the head of security, had every single one of us under strict observation twenty-four hours a day, including me, the other cooks, the waiters, the drivers, and the bodyguards. One time they fired a driver because he gave a lift to someone from the staff in an official car. He wasn't allowed to do that. Go off somewhere in a twosome? They might be trying to conspire.

Whenever I went to my hometown to visit my mother, two agents from the Sigurimi, the secret police, always drove behind me. They followed me quite openly, so every day I used to say "Good morning" to them, and they returned my greeting.

They were followed by two more agents. I knew about them as well. How many agents were following those two? I have no idea. But you can bet there were some.

Whenever the fishermen from Pogradec, where Hoxha had a villa, sailed out to catch fish for him, there were two agents on board with them, and two other boats accompanied them, with nothing but agents on board. They watched the fishermen—and their fellow agents—the whole time through binoculars. At the farms that worked for us, they couldn't even milk the cows without the presence of at least two Sigurimi men to make sure nobody added anything to the milk or the cheese that ended up on Hoxha's table.

In my hometown I preferred not to greet my old friends too effusively, to avoid bringing them under suspicion. Once I spent fifteen minutes chatting with an old school friend. The next day he was summoned by the police. They checked to make sure he wasn't a spy. Luckily, he came from a good family that had served the country well, and they soon let him go.

But I was just an ordinary cook. I wonder how strict an eye they kept on others?

To this day, if someone stares at me, I start to sweat. I feel sure they must know something about me.

2.

His fingers are small, short, and plump, but very agile. For a man of over sixty, he's extremely nimble. It's impossible to take a good photo of him because he never sits still: he's always running about, gesticulating, jumping up and down, plucking, chopping, adding, tasting, putting something in, or taking something out.

It's quite irrelevant anyway, because he's told me to delete all my pictures afterward. He's also told me to keep his first and last names secret, and to alter the circumstances of our meeting so that no one will recognize him. The deal we've made is this: I can write about him, but in a way that won't let anyone work out where he lives or what his real name is. He can be found in the online phone book, but he doesn't want to keep explaining on a daily basis what he was doing for a living while most Albanians were starving. So let's call him Mr. K. Nowadays, Mr. K. and his wife have a small restaurant and hotel in a shabby district of a seaside town, and there's nothing he wants more in life than peace and quiet. Most of his customers are workers from a nearby construction site. He cooks for them, just as he once did for Enver Hoxha, shapes the same meat patties for them as he did for the despot who ruled Albania for almost half a century and made it illegal to practice religion. And then—ping!—a frying pan, a drop of oil, and the patties are done.

I found Mr. K. through Lindita Çela, one of the best investigative journalists in the Balkans. Mr. K. was pleased when we turned up, because he's very sociable and likes to meet new people, though at the same time he was worried, because he's afraid of talking about Hoxha. But he sat us down at a table in his restaurant, made us some fish, squid, and fries, and then sat with us and started to explain his philosophy of cooking.

He says you have to cook naturally.

The answers to any question or challenge, and to all the ills that life throws at us, lie in nature. An allergy? You have to know which food items don't go together. Digestion? Fennel is ideal for purging the blood of excess residue. Diabetes? Oh! That's an interesting topic. Mr. K. has a lot to say about it, so let's leave it for later.

You have to cook with love. If you don't have that love in you, if it's not passing through your hands, it won't be imparted to the meat, vegetables, stock, and mutton that you have to separate from the bone, or the veal (which he happens to be pounding with a ceramic pestle on a eucalyptus chopping board, "because a natural one is always much better than plastic"), or into the apple he's deftly peeling from which, in a few quick moves, he carves the most lifelike bird in the world, with feathers, eyes, wings, and a tail—a bird that looks as if it's just come to a brief stop but is about to rouse itself and fly away from us, out the window. So if you haven't got that love in you, you'd better not take up cooking, but go and do something else entirely.

If he's being sincere, it took Mr. K. a long time to find that love in himself. He wanted to be a mechanic; he was fascinated by cars. But that was in the days when the party made all the decisions. So it was the party, goodness knows why, that decided he'd be a superb cook.

For ages he refused. But there was no arguing with the party. If he wanted to leave home, if he wanted training, he'd have to become a cook.

Only years later did he appreciate how much he'd learned because of his job. Every day he goes to the hillside that we can see from his window and picks fresh herbs. And on the construction site that we can see through the other window, he has cultivated a small garden where he grows tomatoes and cucumbers, as well as basil, salvia, and some other herbs I can't identify.

"I'll take you there," he says, once he has accepted that he is going to talk to me. "The kitchen is a pharmacy. You'll find the answer to all sorts of ailments in your diet. You'll leave my place a much wiser man."

But before we go anywhere, we're going to talk a while. Mr. K. is ready for that now.

I take out my notebook. And we're off.

3.

How did I end up with Comrade Enver? I have no idea. I was working as a cook at a construction site for some engineers from Italy when one day two soldiers came to see me and said I had to pack up, because they were taking me to do another job, in the city of Vlorë, for a whole month.

The trip was very inconvenient for me. My wife was pregnant, and I didn't want to leave her on her own. But when the party decided you were going, you went. Without argument.

In Vlorë they took me to a villa built on a bluff right by the sea, with a beautiful view of the mountains and the bay. There were olive trees and palm trees growing there. I immediately realized I was going to work for someone very important, but for the first few days I didn't know who it was. The chef who was already there had to go to the hospital, so they needed a replacement. She showed me where she kept the pots, and where to find what produce, but she didn't tell me whom I'd be working for. She wasn't allowed to. And I didn't ask.

After a few days, a tall, well-built man came along and said, "Comrade K., you have an extremely important task ahead of you. My name is Sulo Gradeci, and I'm the head of Comrade Enver Hoxha's security. This villa is his holiday home. For the next few weeks you're going to cook here."

My legs turned to jelly. Enver Hoxha. The man who'd been ruling Albania for the past twenty-five years, since before I was born.

So I just stammered that it was an honor for me.

Why had they chosen me? I have no idea. I was young and cheerful, and everyone liked me. Enver liked to have cheerful people around him. Maybe that's what this was about?

I don't remember much about that month in Vlorë. I was far too busy. I'm sure I cooked Albanian dishes, because Hoxha didn't eat any other kind. But what specifically? He loved the cuisine of Gjirokastër, the city where he was born, so I probably tried to make something from those parts. I remember that every day I grilled him a piece of cheese for breakfast, with honey or jam—or, best of all, with orange marmalade.

In that period I only ever saw Hoxha from a distance. But I can't have managed too badly with the cooking, be-

cause after two or three weeks Sulo Gradeci came to see me
again and said that someone wanted to meet me. He took me
into the garden, where Nexhmije Hoxha, Enver's wife, was
sitting at a table. I knew her from our schoolbooks. She had
been with Enver since their days in the partisans; after the
war she'd become head of the Institute of Marxist-Leninist
Studies.

"K.!" she said. "We're very pleased with your cooking."

I bowed.

And then she said, "We're taking you to Tirana with us!"

That was the end of our meeting.

Once again, nobody asked me how I felt about it. That's
how it worked: the party knows what's right and what it expects of you. You don't argue with the party.

So once again I said it was an honor for me, then bowed
and left.

For a while I wondered whether to say that my wife was
pregnant and that I'd like to get in touch with her. For the
past month in Vlorë, I hadn't been able to call her once. But I
figured it was better to ask Sulo Gradeci about that.

And it was the right thing to do. As soon as I brought up
the topic of my wife, Comrade Sulo replied, "It's all been
arranged. The boys from security will take you to Fier. But
remember: You're not allowed to tell anyone whom you're
working for. Not even your wife."

So I told my wife they were transferring me from Vlorë to
Tirana but I had no idea whom I'd be working for. I hugged her,
and I left.

4.

The man who shot Jovan's father in the back of the head was wearing a threadbare gray suit. He refused the offer of alcohol, so Jovan bought him a coffee. He offered him something to eat too, but the man said no. He didn't want to stop for long.

So they sipped coffee and talked, first about politics, then sports and work. The man criticized the government's recent decisions and complained about his health, though Jovan can't remember which decisions he mentioned or what exactly was wrong with him.

But he does remember that the man who shot his father in the back of the head drank his coffee black, without milk. And that he added a teaspoon and a half of sugar.

Jovan is telling me all this at a café in downtown Tirana. As he speaks, he leafs through the menu and chooses a kind of fish for me that he says I absolutely have to try while I'm in Albania, which is, after all, on the Adriatic.

"If you've had sea bream before, why not try John Dory?" he suggests.

I'm finding it hard to get my head around all this information: on the one hand, fish, and, on the other, the tragic story of his father.

"My father loved fish," says Jovan. "Ever since I found that out, I've eaten it several times a week."

"Do you do everything your father did?"

"I try to."

Finally, we order a "Fisherman's Platter": a little of everything. Half an hour later we're served a selection of fish from the Albanian sea, and Jovan's speech is still peppered with the word "father." His name was Koço Plaku. They came for him when Jovan was six months old, in the fall of 1975. He never saw his father again, so he cannot remember his voice, or his face, or the color of his eyes.

Even though Jovan and his mother still live together, she refuses to talk about his father.

"All her life she's been afraid of everything," says Jovan, shaking his head. "I'd rather die than be that scared."

Koço Plaku was a geologist who discovered one of the largest deposits of crude oil in Albania, not far from the city of Fier.

"The state made a lot of money thanks to his discoveries," says Jovan. "Despite that, he was told in court that he was a spy. He was one of the victims of the purges that Hoxha's regime regularly conducted here."

He was sentenced to death.

"My mother and I had to go back to the countryside," Jovan continues. "We had nothing to eat. We were the family of an enemy of the people. Anyone who tried to help us would have been arrested. So I ate soup made of tree bark, and I used to roast frogs on the bonfire. I'd skewer them on a stick like kebabs. The teacher used to hit me for no reason, and shout, 'You'll end up like your father!'"

"How did you cope?"

"I was contrary. The more I was told to hate my own father, the more firmly I promised myself I'd find out all about him when I grew up. And once I had learned how he died, I'd go and find his grave."

5.

To talk about Enver Hoxha, I've arranged to meet Erjon Hysaj, a historian from Tirana. We're sitting in Blloku, once a closed district only for the people in power and now the most fashionable and expensive part of Tirana. We order *byrek*, which is a flaky pie made of puff pastry with meat and cheese inside, and then Erjon starts his account.

"Hoxha was the son of an imam from Gjirokastër, a city in the north of Albania. When World War II broke out, he joined the communist partisans. He soon began to rise up the ranks. Why? Because he was ruthless. He killed everyone who might stand in his way: comrades from his unit, and people who had supported them. He had his own brother-in-law killed, although he had often protected him and put him up for the night at his house."

"Why?"

"Because what mattered to him most was power. He killed anyone who might take it away from him. Anyone who was strong or had people's respect."

After the war, Hoxha was soon the country's unchallenged leader. He collectivized the countryside, dried out the marshes, combated illiteracy, and built factories, all with money from his allies—Yugoslavia at first and later, when he quarreled with Yugoslavia, the Soviet Union. Later still, when he quarreled with the Soviet Union, the money came from China. He wanted to change Albania from a society that was stuck in the Middle Ages (when he took power, 80 percent of the country's citizens lived off agricultural labor, and roughly the same percentage were unable to read or write) into a modern one.

He fought effective campaigns against syphilis, malaria, and lack of education. In the 1930s, average male life expectancy had been forty-two, but thirty years later it had risen to sixty-seven. Within two decades almost all children were going to school, and 90 percent of Albanians had learned to read and write.

But at the same time, Hoxha still went on killing, just as during the war.

"Just after the war he had his own schoolmates, who remembered what a poor student he'd been, killed. And the girls from school who had once refused his advances," says Erjon. "And thousands of others who didn't agree with his heavy-handed policies. He built a system of labor camps and political prisons. About 200,000 people were sent to them. There they were made to work beyond their strength in mines and on construction sites. Many of them died."

During Hoxha's time in office some six thousand people were shot dead.

More and more often, people had nothing to eat. But anyone who publicly stated that there wasn't any meat would end up in a labor camp. In extreme cases they were executed.

6.

I went to live in Blloku, a district to which no outsiders had access. My food went straight to Enver's table, and I was very excited about it. I was a little over twenty, but I'd reached the capital and was cooking for the leader! In addition, after a few months Sulo Gradeci trusted me enough to allow my wife and our daughter, who had been born in the meantime, to come and live with me.

One day I had left the kitchen and gone into the garden for a break, when Enver's son Sokol suddenly appeared.

"K.," he said, "today my father would like to meet you."

"That's a great honor. I'll go and change," I said. "My pants are covered in flour, and my hands are mucky too."

But Sokol just laughed and said, "Too late, he's here already!"

And suddenly Hoxha was there in front of us, as if he'd sprung out of the earth.

I was terrified. I'd heard he was tall, but he was a giant, and as you can see, I am rather small.

"*Mirëdita*," he greeted me, which means "good afternoon" in Albanian. "Allow me to give you some advice. It's not enough to be a good cook, because there are plenty of good cooks. To be really good, you must be inventive and imaginative too. Do you understand what I'm saying? Have a good day."

I bowed and promised I'd try to follow his advice. Enver went off to see to his affairs, and I went back to the kitchen.

But there's one thing you have to remember: This was Enver Hoxha. The leader. Every word he spoke was a command, so "you have to be creative" wasn't a piece of advice. That's how it had to be. If you wanted to live, you had to take every one of his comments to heart.

7.

Sulo Gradeci introduced me to the doctors responsible for Comrade Enver's health: Dr. Fejzi Hoxha, Dr. Isuf Kalo, and Dr. Ylli Popa, who were the best physicians in the country in those days. A few years before I started working for him, Hoxha had had a serious heart attack. Since then, they frequently examined him; even while he was asleep at night, they hooked up their equipment and checked to see if his heart was working well. My duties included preparing coffee and sandwiches for them for these night shifts.

But Hoxha's biggest problem was diabetes. He had been suffering from it for many years and could eat no more than fifteen hundred calories a day. There could be no straying from this rule. Everything had to be measured out, like at a pharmacy.

Once a week I attended the medical consultation. All the doctors stressed the importance of the right diet. They said the state of Hoxha's health depended on my work.

And I knew that my life depended on Hoxha's health. If he were to die, they'd say, "The chef didn't take enough care with his diet." There'd be a trial, a sentence, maybe even death. But I was young, and I had my family to live for.

At their consultations the doctors talked in great detail about how much calcium and potassium Hoxha needed, and how many vitamins. Jointly we considered what I could cook to provide him with all these things while being careful not to exceed the permissible number of calories. I had to translate the numbers they provided into the language of cooking.

To fit everything essential to a man in his prime into less than fifteen hundred calories was extremely tough. Hoxha was big; he was almost six feet five. On top of that, he worked hard every day.

In my view, because of this diet Hoxha spent most of his life feeling hungry, and that's why he was usually agitated. How could that have affected his decisions? Just think what sorts of decisions you would make if you were hungry and in a terrible mood all the time.

I soon learned to recognize what sort of mood he was in

and did my best to adjust accordingly. When I could see that he was angry, I kept that in mind while planning his dinner. On those days I did my best to make something from Gjirokastër, his hometown. We all cheer up when we eat something we remember from childhood, don't we?

So for breakfast, as when I first cooked for him, he had a piece of cheese with jam.

For lunch he had vegetable soup, but not made with a meat stock, because he wasn't allowed that, and then a small piece of veal, lamb, or fish.

For dessert he ate fruit, but not the sweet kind—sour apples or plums.

For supper he had some yogurt.

He hardly ate any bread; the doctors told him those were empty calories, and he dropped the habit entirely.

On the other hand, whenever I saw that he was in a very bad mood, walking down the corridor without noticing anyone or responding to greetings, I knew he needed something extra. So I'd make a dessert. Naturally, I'd make it using sugar for diabetics, just a small portion, and only after consulting his nurse. But I knew that on those days Hoxha needed something sweet. And that it'd be better for all of us, for the entire country, if he was served a dessert.

It worked. I knew how to improve his temper. Quite often he'd sit down at the table feeling agitated and get up in a good mood, joking even. Who knows how many people's lives I saved that way?

Hoxha's nurse was named Kostandina Naumi. She was extremely devoted to her job. We'd compile the menus together, trying hard to make sure everything always tasted good and that nothing was missing from his diet but also taking care not to exceed the permissible number of calories.

Kostandina had been with Enver for many years. She told me how she'd traveled back from the Soviet Union with him in 1960, when he had broken off relations with Khrushchev. Hoxha was afraid the Soviet comrades would try to kill him, so he refused to go home by plane. He, Kostandina, and several others had instead gone from Moscow to Tirana by train, which took over a week. On this journey she had been his cook and had made him an omelet or scrambled eggs each day on a stove fueled by coal provided by the stoker.

Kostandina also tested the food before it ended up on Hoxha's table. There were no other tasters. She would help herself to a little bit of each dish, and we'd wait to make sure that nothing happened to her; when nothing went wrong, the food could be served to Hoxha and his family.

She stuck firmly to her principles, and I never saw her joking or laughing.

8.

The Hoxhas grew very fond of me, especially Enver's wife, Nexhmije. When I had worked for them for several years, they took me to her parents' house with them for New Year's. On that occasion I made a traditional dessert from the city of Peshkopi that's called *sheqerpare*. I made two versions, one with sugar for Nexhmije and her parents and one with special sugar for diabetics for Enver.

Making desserts for him was a risky business. I once made him a different sweet, *hasude*, which is a pudding made with cornstarch, cinnamon, and nuts; naturally, for him I replaced regular sugar with sugar for diabetics. He tried it and sent it back. The waiter repeated his words to me: "This doesn't taste like *hasude* at all. If you're going to make it like that, better not make it at all."

I was horrified. My life could depend on the taste of the dishes I prepared! I started spending long hours in the kitchen, experimenting with sugar for diabetics. I figured out how to use it to make desserts that tasted the same as when you use normal sugar.

Luckily, that time, at New Year's, my *sheqerpare* came out very well. Hoxha even praised me, which rarely happened. And Nexhmije said, "Thank you, K. Come and sit with us for a while."

I refused. Who on earth was I to sit down in the presence of Comrade Enver? But Nexhmije insisted. So I sat down. Thanks to my *sheqerpare* I sat at the same table as Enver and his family on New Year's Eve. Not many of his staff achieved such an honor.

You'd like the recipe? You need three glasses of flour, half a block of butter, three eggs, a glass of sugar, some baking powder, and vanilla. To make it the way I made it for Hoxha, you have to replace the sugar with xylitol, of course. You use these ingredients to make a dough.

For the syrup you need two more glasses of sugar, half a glass of water, and vanilla.

You tip the sugar into a bowl, then melt the butter in a frying pan and pour it into the bowl with the sugar. Add the eggs, vanilla, and flour, and mix until you have a thick yellow dough. Make little balls out of it, arrange them on a baking tray, and bake for twenty minutes at 180 degrees (360 Fahrenheit). Take them out when they start to brown.

Now the syrup. Bring the sugar, vanilla, and half glass of water to a boil in a small saucepan. Once it's boiling, pour it over the dough balls.

I couldn't do this for Hoxha, but it tastes great with whipped cream and fruit.

9.

Nexhmije, Enver Hoxha's wife, is almost one hundred years old. She's living out her days in good health in the suburbs of Tirana.

Lindita Çela, my Albanian friend and guide, has been to see her twice. The first time she was sent by a newspaper whose owner was on good terms with the former apparatchiks.

"She was very polite to me and gave the impression of being a dear old granny," says the journalist.

The second time, Lindita was working for a different newspaper.

"She recognized me, because she has the memory of an elephant. She invited me to come for coffee, and once again she was nice and charming. She started asking how the editor in chief of my old newspaper was doing, so I had to explain that I didn't work there anymore. In a split second she changed into a monster and started screaming, 'So who sent you here? Get out!'"

Even so, we try to go and see her; perhaps she'll be willing to talk to a foreign journalist? We agree that I'll pretend to be a bit on the slow side, and Lindita will do the talking. Just in case, we write a letter too. Saying that I'd like to ask her how she sees today's world. How she views the foreigners who can come here legally and freely now. What she thinks of the grocery stores where you can buy everything. Does she shop there? Does she take advantage of the free market? Does she vote in the elections?

I'd also like to ask if she regrets anything from the time when her husband's people shot other Albanians without trial.

"Nexhmije and her husband have the blood of thousands of people on their hands. She has never apologized to anyone for anything. She always says, 'There were mistakes, distortions; we weren't told about everything.' Like hell! I remember the Albania of my childhood. Every child knew what was going on here, and she didn't? My mother used to make bread out of nettles because there was nothing else to eat," says Lindita angrily.

The dictator's widow lives in a former chicken hatchery converted into a house. The neighbors refer to her as the Old Lady, or just by her first name, Nexhmije. But on the whole they don't talk to her. Oddly enough, Nexhmije happens to live right next door to a family that was sent to a camp when her husband was in power.

We turn into a small, nameless, muddy street, passing a few cars tightly parked, a gate with a vine trailing from its top, and a small garden surrounded by a hedge, in which someone is hauling planks around to build a small bonfire before finally entering a spacious, high-ceilinged passage.

In it a quilt has been spread out to dry—Nexhmije Hoxha's quilt.

By the door there's a pair of ladies' shoes—Nexhmije Hoxha's shoes.

Next to the shoes there's a laundry rack—Nexhmije Hoxha's laundry rack. There are some pillowcases drying on it—also hers.

From the bits and pieces set out on the gallery, I can see that the former dictator's wife lives modestly and is inclined to accumulate unnecessary clutter.

We're standing at the door. Ding-dong.

A woman of about sixty opens it (we soon learn that this is her daughter, Pranvera). Lindita politely explains who we are. Pranvera listens and nods. I take advantage of these few seconds to inspect the apartment, but all I can see is a large bookcase. Everything else is shielded by the kind of curtain you hang up to keep out flies.

Suddenly behind this curtain I see the silhouette of an old woman. White hair swept up in a bun. A skirt straight from a school for well-bred young ladies. A sweater. But I can't see her eyes; all I can see are some thick eyeglass frames.

Yes, it's her. Nexhmije Hoxha. The wife of Enver, the last Stalinist in Europe and the world. The woman who shares his responsibility for the deaths of thousands.

For a moment she stands there looking at me.

And I'm looking at her.

It lasts only an instant, but it makes me feel uneasy.

Meanwhile, Pranvera politely but firmly refuses to let us in to see her.

10.

I didn't cook fancy food for Hoxha, and he didn't expect me to. Of course he liked good food, but at the same time he and Nexhmije were quite stingy; they counted every penny before spending it, even though it was state money. Anyway, Nexhmije mainly ate carrots; she had a problem with her gallbladder, and that's what the doctors recommended.

Hoxha and his family ate the typical Albanian dishes everyone in our country knows. If anything was different about their household, it was that they had the opportunity to employ good cooks, who knew how to bring their own style to the food. What was special about my style? I liked to experiment with seasoning. The seasoning for a dish is like makeup for a woman; it can bring out flavors you'd never suspect were there.

I also had a flair for decoration. Instead of serving Hoxha a typically sliced raw apple, I'd cut a notch in the last bit of peel, use a seed to make an eye, and serve it to him in the shape of a bird. For one of his sons' birthdays, I served a roast suckling pig that was wearing a hat and had a lit cigarette in its mouth. Hoxha enjoyed that sort of little joke. The whole family remembered that pig for years.

I had to be at my most imaginative when Hoxha quarreled with the Chinese and then spent the last few years of his rule running Albania in total isolation. In those days, even we sometimes ran out of milk or meat. For a cook that's a disaster. But I never said a dish wouldn't work or couldn't be made. I'd have regarded that as a failure. If an ingredient was missing, I did my best to replace it with something else.

One time, for instance, we'd gone to the mountains, and on the way it turned out the bodyguards had forgotten to bring the desserts we'd prepared in advance. What could we do? Go back? Impossible. But if there were no desserts, everyone would be upset!

So I got hold of some apples, pureed some of them with several spoonfuls of honey in a blender, and baked the rest. I cored the baked ones and poured the apple-and-honey mousse into the holes I'd made. Hoxha was delighted. "How do you know this recipe?" he asked. To which I said, "There's no such recipe. I just had to do something."

I found similar ways to cope with deficit items, unavailable in Albania. One time Hoxha summoned me and said, "When I was a student in France, I ate a delicious salad that had roasted chestnuts in it. Make me one like that." One of his assistants brought me a very fine cookbook from Hoxha's own library; he must have been interested in cuisine to have bought a book like that one.

So we ordered some chestnuts. But as so often in the communist era, someone failed to do their job: several months went by before the chestnuts arrived, and in the meantime they'd gone moldy. What was I to do? Tell Hoxha the chestnuts had gone bad because some idiot hadn't looked after them before they got here? Tell him they don't grow in our country—though they could—because no one had ever thought of planting them?

No way. So there I was, and there was Hoxha. To him, I was the man responsible for the food on the table; he didn't want to hear what had happened to the chestnuts on the way. All he wanted to know was where was the roasted chestnut salad he'd ordered me to make?

So I roasted the moldy chestnuts, peeled them, and . . . threw them all away. If I had served them to him, they'd definitely have thought I was trying to poison him. I replaced them with hazelnuts, which I shelled and halved, then added some olive oil, cooked them in milk, and decorated the salad with rose petals. I can't remember the recipe well, but I did exactly what it said.

Hoxha never asked about the chestnuts. Maybe the hazelnut

salad tasted good enough for him to forget about them? Or
perhaps he realized that in his country lots of things were un-
obtainable, even for the leader? I think it must have been frus-
trating for him, but that was the situation.

Another time he remembered that in France he had eaten
seedless grapes. Perhaps he had, but that sort of grape didn't
grow in Albania, at least not on a trusted farm. So what did I
do? What else could I do? I sat there picking the seeds out of
one grape after another.

11.

Enver Hoxha died in 1985. A few years later the winds of democratic change reached Albania from Poland and Germany. But
while the Poles were electing their first noncommunist government, and the Germans were toppling the Berlin Wall, Hoxha's successor, Ramiz Alia, was explaining to the Albanians that life in
those countries was changing for the worse. Albanian television
showed fake footage of Poles, Germans, and Hungarians dying in
the streets of hunger.

"But we were the ones dying," says Jovan, with a bitter smile.

Finally, in the spring of 1991, the first democratic elections were
held in Albania too.

Jovan had never forgotten that he'd sworn to find his father's
grave. Soon after that election he made an application to the Ministry of Internal Affairs for the declassification of the trial documents of the engineer Plaku. He also asked to be shown his burial
site. He thought that now, in the new era, it would be simple.

For a long time there was no reply.

"I kept going to the ministry, making inquiries, and being insistent," he says. "Finally I received an official letter with more than a dozen stamps, which said, 'The documentation relating to your father has been destroyed.'"

But Jovan refused to give in. When the official route failed, he used his most effective weapon: his personal charm. And also money. He had some, because in the early 1990s he'd set up a construction firm that won several major commissions in Tirana.

And a miracle occurred. Several months later, forty volumes of documents and a dozen tapes from the trial were found. So now, as an adult, Jovan switched on the tape recorder and heard his father's voice for the first time in his life, saying, "I am innocent."

12.

Working for Enver gave me tremendous satisfaction, and I learned a huge amount because of my job. But I lived in a constant state of fear. Everyone on the staff was afraid that one day Enver would get up in a bad mood and have us all sent to a camp or have us killed. Maybe Kostandina, the nurse, and Sulo Gradeci, the head of security, weren't afraid; they were indispensable to him. But what about the rest of us? There were hundreds of cooks like me. We were all easily replaceable.

Hoxha's first cook had committed suicide. I never found out why. Later, one of the cooks who began to work for him long before I did disappeared. I don't know what happened to him; one day he just didn't come to work, and it was better not to ask where he'd gone.

But I wanted to live.

I thought long and hard about what I could do to come out of Enver Hoxha's kitchen alive. And then I had an idea.

I already knew how to improve his mood: I only had to cook something from Gjirokastër, or make a dessert. But I was doing it according to cookbooks when I should have been making his meals the way Hoxha's mother had cooked for him when he was a little boy. His mother was no longer alive, and I knew he missed her very much.

I needed to replace her.

That was my idea, though I knew it was an insolent, brazen one: if I replaced his mother, then he couldn't kill me.

Easily said, right? But how was I to do it? After all, I couldn't go and ask Hoxha, "Comrade Enver, how exactly did your mother do the cooking? Can you give me a few hints?"

Luckily, in those days Enver's sister Sano was living with him. They'd been raised together in the same house. Sano had been taught how to cook by her mother from early childhood. What's more, she was very kindhearted, and she loved her brother dearly.

So I went to see her and said, "Comrade, I'd like to make my cooking as delicious as possible for Comrade Enver. It occurred to me that you might be able to help."

And I explained what I had in mind, stressing Enver's happiness, of course, not the fact that I was afraid for my life.

Sano agreed.

13.

In his father's case files, Jovan found some names, which he looked up in the phone book. He called and made appointments.

"It was dreadful," he says, when there's nothing left of our fish but bones. "While I was eating frogs, those people had plenty of money and good food. But I gritted my teeth and went on talking to them. If they agreed, I met up with them and we drank *rakiah* together. Once they were a bit drunk, they started telling me how they'd killed people. They joked about it. I often felt like getting up and screaming, but I had to control myself. I had to find my father's grave, and screaming wouldn't have helped. So I drank with them, listened, and tried to memorize as much as I could."

A few years later Jovan succeeded in getting hold of Koço Plaku's execution file.

"There were four signatures. The first belonged to the coroner, who had signed the death certificate in absentia, so there was no point talking to him. Two of the agents who had signed the document had died since. But the third one was still alive. The one who had shot my father in the back of the head."

It took Jovan several weeks to gather the strength to call.

First, he drove to the former agent's apartment block. Through the car window he watched a shriveled old man in a gray suit who went to the local café every day. Finally, he took out his phone. He was quite prepared for the guy to tell him to go to hell, but amazingly he agreed to meet with him.

Jovan arrived ahead of time. He was so nervous that he smoked half a pack of cigarettes. But the old man in the gray suit was as cool as a cucumber.

"We talked about all those unnecessary things, such as politics and sports, until I finally got to the point. I asked him, 'Where did you kill my father? I want to find his remains and bury them.'"

The old man was very polite. He said of course he remembered the engineer Plaku, but he couldn't remember where he had shot him. "We worked at a large number of sites." When Jovan tried to press him, the man threw up his hands helplessly. And at the end of the conversation, as if trying to console Jovan, he said, "Mr. Plaku, we are all victims of that dreadful system."

"That was the one and only moment when I felt like punching him in the face," says Jovan. "Him? A victim? How the fuck was he a victim? I felt as if he'd slapped me."

"Then what?" I ask.

"That was that. It went on for a while. I don't want revenge on anyone. I just want to find my father's grave."

So Jovan shook the hand of the man who had shot his father in the back of the head, and went on with his search.

He still hasn't found the place where his father was killed.

14.

Sano taught me how to make *shapkat*, *kofte*, and *gahi*—all in exactly the way they were made in Gjirokastër. She showed me exactly how much flour, salt, and spices their mother would have added. She also taught me to make *tarhana*—a Turkish soup that he liked to have for breakfast. He was very happy to eat it with tomatoes and onions on cold, rainy days.

Along the way she told me about their life. How their father had gone abroad with their older brother, and she and her mother and siblings had moved into their uncle's house. How Enver had left for college in France. How he had come back and got involved with the partisans. How he used to come home secretly now and then. And how proud their mother had been when he became leader of the entire country. Sano gave me a real lesson in the history of Albania, except that it was told at the kitchen table.

Occasionally, Sano cooked with me for an hour or more; then she'd go to her room, change for supper, and casually come downstairs to dine with Enver and his family. She didn't bat an eyelid as Enver chowed down on the food we'd prepared together. Apparently, several times he said, "Sano, how did he make this *shapkat*? It tastes just the same as it did at home!"

And Sano would keep very quiet. She never let on to him that she had taught me.

But Nexhmije knew the truth. She was pleased with me. She took great care of Enver and very often showed me that she appreciated what I was doing for her husband. Thanks to her I was their favorite cook. I achieved my goal; now it was impossible to replace me with anyone else.

Plenty of people failed to survive Hoxha's regime, including his prime minister and closest friend, Mehmet Shehu.

But I survived.

Thanks to my cooking. And thanks to Enver, who said I must be inventive and imaginative.

Snack

អាហារសម្រន់

The Organization? Okay, one thing at a time.

My parents came from a small village in Kampong Cham province. I had two sisters and six brothers. The oldest was named Yung San, and he became a teacher at a middle school in a town named Skuon. Our parents spent all their savings on his education. We were very proud of him.

My mother used to weave mats, hammocks, and mosquito nets, and my father would pack everything she had made into a large bag and take it to the market in the city to sell. While he was gone, my mother would roll tobacco to make cigarettes that she sold in the village, and she also hired herself out as a cook for wedding parties. She worked very hard.

When I was twelve, my father died, and my mother sent me to live with my brother in Skuon. That meant I could go to school. My father had preferred me to stay home and help my mother to weave hammocks.

In Skuon it turned out that my brother was going to secret meetings after work. I was curious about them. I kept pestering him to tell me about them, but he insisted that he couldn't tell a little girl. Then, once I had grown up a bit, he started to test me. For instance, he'd say that Cambodian peasants work beyond their strength and workers are dying in the factories. And he'd wait to see how I'd respond. These words affected me; several times I burst into tears. I agreed with everything he said.

So once I had finished school, my brother took me to a meeting with our cousin Koy Thuon. He was one of the sweetest people I've ever met. He said he already knew my views and that there was an organization that wanted to change Cambodia to make people's lives better. Then I learned that Koy Thuon and my brother belonged to this organization, and its meetings were the ones they'd both been secretly attending.

Koy Thuon told me a lot of things. "When we liberate the country," he said, "there will be plenty of food for everyone."

It was a beautiful vision. Imagine a regime in which the soldiers rob the people. Imagine children whose bellies are swollen with hunger. And then imagine someone saying, "There can be enough food for everyone."

THERE CAN BE ENOUGH FOOD FOR EVERYONE.

Anyone who has a heart would want to help an organization like that!

So when Koy Thuon said I could be helpful and that sometimes, as a courier, I could carry something—a letter or a parcel—from place to place, I didn't hesitate. "Yes, I want to help," I said.

That's how I joined Angkar.

Ever since, Angkar is me.

I am Angkar.

Soon after, we set off for the guerrilla base in Ratanakiri province. I went with my brother Yung San, my cousin Koy

Thuon, and one other comrade. We walked through the jungle for almost a month. We didn't stop at any of the villages, because we could have run into soldiers there. We mostly ate wild fruits, and my comrades sometimes hunted birds.

Ratanakiri is a very wild part of the country; it's a region inhabited by many tribes who live as they did centuries ago. These people, the Khmer Loeu, wear traditional costumes and ride elephants; they aren't familiar with cars. From the very start, when Pol Pot first went to live in the jungle, in 1963, they were keen supporters of his movement. At least a dozen of them became his personal bodyguards. I can remember the names of several of those tribes—Pnong, Tampuan, Kuy, Jarai. And I remember how amazed I was by their elephants. The pen for these animals was some distance from the base so that they wouldn't wake us up with their trumpeting, and also so that they wouldn't trample us if something made them panic.

The Khmer Loeu were experts at breaking in elephants. They used them whenever they needed to carry something heavy or transfer the entire base, because that sometimes happened too.

It was the first time I'd been so far from home. I was young; I was doing something good. Life was beautiful.

Supper
Cena

Fish in Mango Sauce

The Story of Erasmo and Flores,
Fidel Castro's Chefs

1.

Erasmo

Boys, grab a seat and give me a while. You can see what's up. They've brought me a swordfish, and I've got to cut it up myself, because the guys in the kitchen will make a hash of it. Get yourselves a coffee and a cookie and wait for me. Or you know what, I'd like a coffee too. The swordfish will keep. So come on, Witold, fire away. First question.

The revolution? Okay, I'll tell you.

The revolution . . .

When I was sixteen, a rumor started going around that a revolution had erupted in the Sierra Maestra and that it was a great thing, led by a man whose name was Fidel.

These stories sounded like fairy tales: Fidel and a few good friends had stood up to Batista's regime. We all hated the dictator Batista, because he never gave us a thought; all he cared about was how to let the American Mafia make as much money from Cuba as possible. And here was Fidel, fighting against Batista on equal terms, setting ambushes for his soldiers in the Sierra Maestra. People were singing songs about him. They admired him. His was a truly incredible story.

At the time I was working at a restaurant in Santa Clara, my hometown. Part of the time I waited tables, and part of the time I helped the chefs, because I'd always been interested in cooking. Everyone at the restaurant, from the owner down to the dishwashers, talked about Castro nonstop. One time they'd say he was dead, because that's what they'd said on the radio, and later that he was alive after all and still fighting, then later on again that he was calling on all of Cuba to go on strike. It made us feel excited, but few people seriously thought of leaving their family and going in search of the guerrillas in the jungle.

I wouldn't have gone either, if not for my best friend in those days. He knew the brothers Rogelio and Enrique Acevedo, who had joined the revolution much earlier, and he said that if we managed to find them, they'd welcome us with open arms.

I wasn't sure about going. But my friend kept bothering me. Until one day he found out that the guerrillas were getting closer to Santa Clara; apparently some of them, including the Acevedo brothers, had moved from the Sierra Maestra to the Sierra del Escambray, a range of mountains not far from our town. To reach the Sierra Maestra, we'd have had to walk almost all the way across Cuba, which would have been very dangerous.

The Escambray Mountains were only two days away.

You're sixteen years old; you're still a boy. So all this sounds like a grand adventure!

Except that my mom was terrified that something might happen to me, and refused to let me join the revolution.

I said all right, I agreed with her, I wasn't going anywhere, and then one night my friend and I simply sneaked out of our houses and ran away. I was sorry I'd had to lie to her, but it was my only option.

On the way we had to be very careful, because there were soldiers on guard everywhere, just waiting for guys like us, heading for Escambray to fight against them. By then they could tell they were going to lose, so they were being extremely brutal. They were killing anyone they suspected of supporting Fidel; people were being killed at night, and then their mutilated bodies were found.

I remember crossing a river that was flooding. And being so badly eaten alive by mosquitoes during the night that it was impossible to get a wink of sleep. To find the guerrillas, we had to question the local peasants, but with caution, because they might report us to the soldiers. Finally, we did it; we found the base.

My friend asked for the Acevedos. They came along, and they really did welcome us like family. They were slim, not much older than us, cheerful, with rifles slung over their shoulders. It made a great impression on me. They embraced my friend, and me, too, while they were at it. At once they found us mess tins and poured us some soup, because we were as hungry as wolves. Once we'd eaten, they took us to see Che Guevara. He was their commander. He was preparing to fight for our hometown, Santa Clara, the most important clash in the revolution, because its capture would open the road to Havana.

Che took a look at us, shook our hands, clapped my friend on the shoulder, and disappeared. He was always running to be somewhere and never had time for anything. Then the Acevedo brothers drove us to Caballete de Casas, where the general staff was located.

The brothers took us into their unit. I remember one of the first questions they asked us: "Got any salt?"

We didn't have any.

One of them gave us a little of his. He said the food here tasted bad and that without salt it was impossible to eat.

Che has been dead for a long time now; he was captured and shot in the war in Bolivia. Both Acevedos are generals; one of them has been a deputy minister. They sometimes come to my restaurant. Then we lock the doors, open a bottle of rum, and talk about old times. But in those days they were teenagers, and Che was an Argentine, deeply involved in our revolution, who had met Fidel in Mexico and come to help him fight for a better world.

I can tell you that everything I did later, under Fidel's command, was a breeze compared with the way Che drove us into the ground. He was hellishly demanding. If he didn't like something, he sure could rip you a new one. If Fidel criticized you, he did it calmly, and that meant you had a chance to put things right. Because if something went wrong, and he didn't say anything, you didn't get a second chance.

But at that point I didn't know Fidel yet; I just heard them talking about him all the time. *El Comandante*, the commandant. Or *el Jefe*, the chief, the leader. There was always someone talking about him, saying how brave he was, what a great speaker he was. I was jealous of anyone who'd met him. Who'd have thought I'd spend more than half my life with him? That he'd become closer to me than my own father? I never expected it.

2.

They drink rum, play cards, whistle for their dogs, pick their noses, and stand in line: for cabs, for fish, for sugar or flour. Rickety old cars ferry them around to the more remote parts of the city, where prostitutes mingle with nuns, fishermen with book dealers, and loving couples with people who never get so much as a hug these days. They sell flowers, cut hair, and buy meat, or just a bone, or just the feet of a chicken.

"I know how to make a delicious soup out of them!" says the old woman whose photograph I take as she carries this particular trophy home. "Drop by and you can try it!"

We smile at each other, though when it occurs to me that she's probably eaten nothing better since the revolution, my smile fades.

I like mingling with the crowd in Havana. Walking with the people among the decaying teeth of the apartment houses, dozens of which collapse each year, or among the markets, where limp chickens are mixed in with plump tomatoes and mangoes. I like to stand in the square with the Cubans where they connect via the internet with their family members who've run off to Miami (the internet and Wi-Fi hot spots operate in just a few places in Havana, and they're astronomically expensive). They show each other their kids and inquire after each other's health, jobs, grandmas, and grandpas. They often laugh while they're having these conversations.

They often cry too. For beneath the surface coating of rum, samba, and cigars are thousands of tragedies.

Also beneath the surface are the secret police, keeping check on the journalists who come here and the Cubans who want to talk to them. The first time I was in Havana, in 2006, I sat down on a bench in the park near the Capitol, which is a copy of the one in Washington and a memento of the days when Cuba and the United States were close. Evening had set in, and the birds were singing like mad. An old man sat down next to me; he was in a threadbare suit and looked like a retired office clerk or accountant. I sat at one end of the bench, and he at the other. Without looking at me, he nodded his head and said, "We live like animals here."

And suddenly two plainclothes policemen came crawling out of the bushes, straight toward us. They asked for our IDs. They handed back my passport and told me to leave. They took the old man away with them. When I tried to protest, I was pushed away with force. I have no idea what happened to him.

So when I went to Cuba to look for Fidel Castro's cook, I knew I had to be careful. I had to watch out for myself and for the people with whom I was going to speak.

Then Barack Obama came to my aid by making a historic trip to Cuba in the spring of 2016, the first such visit since Fidel's revolution.

"Go there at the same time as him," advised my friend Juan, a Cuban who lives in Poland. "All our spooks will be busy chasing spooks from the States. They won't have time to bother with you."

Maybe he was right. So I landed in Havana exactly a week before Obama's visit.

Havana had changed a lot since my previous stay; it was full of new cafés, and at the trendiest bar there was now a nameplate from the community Revolutionary Defense Committee hanging right by the restroom door. Only a few years earlier, when all Cubans were obliged to defend the benefits of the revolution, it would have been unthinkable to associate it with the restroom. I traveled around freely by cab—in the past I could use only the ones that were licensed to carry foreigners—and my one concern was how to avoid being fleeced, because the Cubans were trying every which way to close the economic gap between them and the rest of the world. I could talk to anyone I liked, nobody arrested any old men, and people often criticized the Castro brothers boldly and directly. I found it all surprising.

"As long as you merely criticize but don't try to change anything, they won't get involved," explains Miguel, a friend of a friend, whose father was a senior Communist Party activist in Havana. "Few people still have the strength or the desire to defend socialism. I certainly don't."

Thanks to his late father, Miguel has lots of contacts. He's helping me to find Fidel's chef.

"Best to look via other chefs," he suggests.

He's right.

So we go out to dinner at one of the best restaurants in Havana. We tuck into delicious beef and vegetables, surrounded by colonial furniture and the smoke from expensive cigars, and when we're done, Miguel invites the owner to our table, a man whom, he assures me, he has known forever.

"This señor," he says, pointing at me, "is my friend. He's looking for a cook to interview him, *el Jefe*. You've got to help us."

The owner looks at me, then at Miguel, then starts looking around him, as if to check that there aren't any plainclothes policemen on the other side of the wall, ready to drag him away like the old man I met in the park near the Capitol.

"But that's confidential," he finally says, sighing. "Your friend should write a letter to the ministry."

"A letter? What do you mean?" says Miguel, bursting into laughter. "You know all the cooks in Havana. You are our letter."

"But what if not all the cooks in Havana want to be identified?" says the restaurateur cryptically.

Perhaps Miguel's relaxed attitude is catching, because after they swap a few unnecessary remarks about the price of fuel, the produce at the local market, and various models of cell phone, the owner stops looking over his shoulder.

They chat a while longer, until a bottle of rum appears. After the second glass, the owner relaxes entirely and remembers that Fidel's former chef has opened a restaurant in Old Havana. And after a third glass, he remembers that Fidel's chef has given interviews before now (it's true, I've read them myself, but they didn't include an address), so our meeting shouldn't put him in any danger. And after the fourth glass, he becomes a vocal advocate for my meeting with him.

"Say I sent you!" He's almost shouting. "Or else . . ." There's a long pause. "Take one of my waiters. They were at the same school; it'll be easier for you to talk. Jorge! Jooorgeee!! Come here a moment."

Jorge is twenty-three, with the smile of a Latin matinee idol, and he's so friendly that you start to like him before he's even said anything.

"He's the favorite waiter of all the American tour groups," says the owner, smiling.

And because there aren't any large tour groups on the schedule today, Jorge takes off his apron, and we're off to see Castro's former chef.

His restaurant is named Mama Inés, and it's located in an elegantly restored colonial building. Erasmo Hernandez, as Fidel's former cook is named, wears glasses in fashionable red frames and a scruffy shirt, and when we arrive, he's sitting outside, drinking black coffee. I'm not sure if he'll feel like talking to us, but before he knows it, Jorge is working his charm on him, mentioning various friends they have in common, including several distant relatives. Soon they're talking as if there weren't a fifty-year age gap between them, but as if they'd been to the same culinary school in the same year and had celebrated the end of exams together with cheap rum on Havana's famous avenue, the Malecón.

The conversation goes so well that the next day Jorge asks his boss for a few days off and starts escorting me to my daily meetings with Erasmo. We spend our mornings talking to Castro's former chef, and in the afternoons Jorge seeks out other people who might have something to tell me about Fidel or about Cuban cuisine.

3.

Erasmo

I knew I wanted to cook from the start, probably because I'd worked in a restaurant before then. In our unit there was a real cook, whose name was Castañera. Whenever I had a spare moment, I went to see him, and I questioned him about how to make various things. He'd cooked at a very expensive restaurant before then; he'd joined the revolution because he'd fallen afoul of one of Batista's men. We ate what there was, mainly *ajiaco*, which is a very popular soup in Cuba. Everyone knows how to make it. I used to make it with Castañera almost every day. You take sausage, bacon, chicken, or a pig's head—whatever you can use to make a stock. Once that's ready, you add beans, corn, potatoes, sausage, rice, tomatoes—whatever you have on hand. You can also add fish or shellfish, but in the mountains we very rarely had fish, never mind lobster or shrimp. You toss it all in the pot. And you cook it on a slow flame for about half an hour.

It's delicious, and also very nourishing, so it was ideal for the soldiers.

Che ate the same as everyone else. He never turned his nose up at the food, even though he was from a rich family and must have been used to good food. Castañera would probably have known how to make a dish from his home country, but there was no question of Che eating anything different from the ordinary soldiers.

The one thing that singled him out was his love of black beans. He could eat an entire big bowl of them.

Finally, a few weeks later, we set off toward Santa Clara. I took part in all the major battles in that campaign. I fought at Caibarién and Camajuaní, where Batista's men ran away from us without firing a single shot.

My hometown fell a day later. It happened so fast that some of our comrades sensed a trap. But there was no trap; the road to Havana was open to us. Batista was well aware of this, because a few hours later he fled to the United States. There was so much going on that I didn't have the time to visit my parents.

After the Battle of Santa Clara, Rogelio Acevedo was promoted to captain and Enrique to lieutenant. We all went to Havana. I was shown appreciation too; Che took me into his personal bodyguard.

But I didn't work for him long. You want to know how I ended up with Fidel? Just a moment, I really must deal with that swordfish. Bear with me a while. I'll tell the waiter to bring you some more coffee.

And so our days go by. In the morning there's coffee and conversation, sometimes cooking with Erasmo, whom we gradually befriend. In the afternoon, there are Jorge's acquaintances from culinary school.

Until one day Jorge tells me something truly extraordinary. He has learned from his fellow students about another man who cooked for Castro, named Flores. Not only has this man failed to open his own restaurant since retiring, but he hasn't done at all well either, and is living out his days in isolation and extreme poverty.

There's only one catch: the man has lost his wits.

"Do you want to meet him?" asks Jorge. "I have no idea if he can tell us anything."

Yes, I do want to meet him.

So one of the rattletrap cabs takes us to the outskirts of the city, beyond the marina from where Ernest Hemingway set sail to fish for marlin. We find Flores in a tumbledown house where the plaster is falling off the moldering walls. There are cockroaches the size of a grown man's thumb running around the kitchen, and instead of furniture there are two old armchairs, a legless table, and a television set that stopped working years ago.

Flores is incapable of finishing a story, or even of counting up to ten. He starts on one theme, loses track of it, then starts on another, only to lose track again. The one thing to feature consistently in all his statements is his great love of Fidel. And his fear. That *they'll* come. They, meaning who? For what purpose? Why? He refuses to say.

To go from Erasmo's house to the place where Flores lives is to see a big jump between two different Cubas. Erasmo's Cuba wears brightly colored spectacle frames and fashionable clothes, earns money, and dreams of earning even more. Flores's Cuba dreams of having something to put in the pot. And of not running out of cigarettes. Or at least cigarette butts.

4.

Flores

... What do you want to know? About my mom? All right ...

... My mom was a washerwoman, and my father was better off than she was; his family would never have agreed to the wedding. My granddaddy traded sugarcane with the Americans, he made really good money, so when it turned out my father wanted to marry an ordinary, simple woman who didn't have a dowry, my granddaddy was furious and started shouting. You have to know that my father was very stubborn, but when ...

... when one day I was sitting in a tree that I'd climbed to pick mangoes. I had one in my hands, an extremely fine piece of fruit it was, and I was wondering how to climb down without bruising it, when a column of army vehicles appeared ...

... the vehicles stopped by the tree, I was about fourteen or so at the time. I was still a little punk, an adolescent, and a bearded man got out of one of them, dressed in a uniform the color of an olive and holding a gun, and he asked me my name. "Flores, sir," I said, "my name is Flores," to which he said I had a fine piece of fruit there; then he paused, and I knew that if they wanted to, they could take that mango off me, that I'd never be able to escape from them, and anyway how the hell was I gonna run away from a gang of armed guerrillas? So I quickly said, "I'm happy for you to have it, sir," and I climbed down from the tree, then he smiled, took the mango from me, and said, "You're not giving it to me, but to the revolution," and then he asked, "Flores, my boy, do you know how to read and write?" "No, sir," I replied, "I don't," to which he said, "Flores, my boy, we want to change Cuba so that you can go to school to learn to read and write, and maybe in the future you can be a doctor or a minister."

... I liked that very much, and I said aloud that it wasn't a bad idea, and the man's bodyguards smiled at me in a friendly way, but when ...

... when I stood outside *el Comandante*'s door for the first time, I had a bag of wood on my back for the stove, and I had to lean forward to pass under the low beam, like him, I thought, like *el Comandante* has to lean forward to go in there, seeing as he's much taller than I am. And when the door opened, he was standing in it, Fidel Castro, in his pajamas. "Mind your head," he said, laughing, and pulled my cap down over my ears, "Yes, sir, *Comandante*, I'll be careful," I said, and tossed the wood beside the hearth and began to cook the meal, that day I was to roast him a turkey, meanwhile he

lit a cigar and watched me, he was curious to see how I'd deal
with the turkey, but . . .

. . . but it worries me, and makes me wonder, my friend,
why have the Americans started coming to Cuba now? Why
are they flying their planes here and sailing their ships here?
Why do we agree to that when everyone, when the whole
world knows that it's like in baseball—it all depends on who
throws the first ball, so why do we let them throw the first
ball? Why do we let them win the match before it has really
gotten started?

That's all I can say.

I can't say more. I can't, or they'll come for me. I'd rather
they didn't come.

5.

"I know people who've never stopped saying how much they hate
Fidel, but when he died, they cried like babies."

Miguel, my friend from Havana, is scrutinizing me, as if trying
to make sure I understand what extraordinary people he knows.
We're sitting in his swanky apartment, looking out at a panoramic
view of Havana while enjoying a glass of rum, which Miguel con-
sumes the way most people drink water.

Miguel is from a family of communists, but these days he belongs to the new, part-time-capitalist Cuban middle class. He owns
several apartments, which he bought for peanuts thanks to his
connections, and he rents them out to tourists.

"One of them paid for itself in six months. Another in ten." The
smile of a well-fed cat appears on his face.

I believe he's telling the truth. These days Cuba is the land of milk and honey for anyone with his connections.

"Of course I have to share the profits with several other people," he adds. "Such as the guy who helped me to find apartments at that price. And the guy who gave me permission to buy them. But it was worth it. I'm doing well, and so are they."

Miguel likes to talk about politics. He's well up on them. His father personally knew Fidel and his brother Raúl, who is Cuba's president as we speak.

"I also know old communists who curse the Castro brothers when they think no one's listening." Returning to the main topic, once again he's trying to read my face, to find out if I truly appreciate the weight of what he's telling me. I must have passed the test, because he goes on: "Why? Because in their view Fidel warped the ideal they believed in. Because it ceased to be their revolution, it was the Fidelution instead. Every single person you ask will give you a different opinion. One thing's for sure: he had a truly Caribbean character." At this point Miguel bursts out laughing.

He's right. Fidel's character was evident from childhood. According to his biographers, at an early age he made a bet with his schoolmates: He'd ride a bicycle at high speed into a stone wall. He picked up speed and . . . wham! Seconds later he was lying on the ground with a concussion. Why on earth did he do it? He probably had no idea.

Later in his life there was a whole series of episodes combining bravado with pointless risk. That's what happened on July 26, 1953, when at the head of a hundred-man unit he attacked the Moncada Barracks in the city of Santiago de Cuba.

"They were badly prepared, with no weapons. They didn't stand a chance," says Miguel. "Most of them ended up dead or in jail."

Fidel was imprisoned on Isla de Pinos, where he killed time by cooking spaghetti on a small electric plate. He mastered this art to perfection. For many years it was his signature dish.

On his release, he was ordered to leave the country. He ended up in Mexico, but he wasn't interested in exile, so at the first opportunity he loaded eighty-two comrades onto the twelve-man yacht *Granma*, and—once again with great bravado—headed back to Cuba. Che Guevara describes in his memoirs how they spent almost the entire journey being seasick and finally almost died of hunger because the voyage went on for several days longer than planned.* Fidel came close to killing his own first comrades before the revolution had actually started.

Luckily, the local farmers and *carboneros* (who make charcoal) received the band of ragamuffins from the *Granma* extremely well; they fed them and allowed them to buy provisions for the journey. From there Castro and his gang pressed onward, into the Sierra Maestra. And again—with just a dozen or so armed guerrillas under him—Castro challenged Fulgencio Batista, who had a well-equipped army and the support of the powerful United States at his disposal.

There were so few of them that in February 1957 they ran around the hut where the *New York Times* correspondent Herbert Matthews was talking to Fidel, to give Matthews the impression that he was watching the exercises of a large group of soldiers.

Batista sent ten thousand soldiers to fight the rebels.

But Fidel Castro never calculated his chances. Once again, as on his bicycle, he rode at full speed toward the wall. He was convinced he'd win. And that history would admit he was right.

---

* Che Guevara, *Che: The Diaries of Ernesto Che Guevara*, trans. Alexandra Keeble (Ocean Press, 2008), 37.

And it did. At least for several decades.

Batista's soldiers felt uneasy in the mountains, where the guerrillas kept ambushing them. Their numbers diminished by the day. Until 1958 when Fidel shifted to the offensive and in early 1959 entered Havana in triumph.

6.

Erasmo

I met Fidel a few days after we entered the capital, at the house of Antonio Núñez Jiménez, a scientist who would later be the first Cuban to sail to the Antarctic. Jiménez had been in Che's unit too and then became head of the National Institute for Agrarian Reform. The meeting at his house had to do with that reform, and along the way it turned out Fidel needed someone for security. Che adored Fidel and wanted to share everything he had with him, so without a second thought he told me to transfer to Castro's bodyguards. Was I pleased? Of course! Not only had I finally met Fidel; I'd started working with him too.

I spent several years walking behind him—fetch this, take that, let's go here, let's go there. But although we were working for the chief, no one ever thought about food. There was always something more important. I was the first to think about the fact that the chief went about hungry, so one day I just set up a cooking pot and something to go in it and then made a campfire, and once *El Jefe* had finished his meeting, there was soup ready for him. It wasn't part of my duties, but I'd always liked to cook, and that way I didn't go hungry either.

Fidel liked this idea, so I did the same thing more often.

In time I started taking the pot with me wherever we went. We often worked right around the clock; Fidel would invite guests, or he'd stay up late with someone, or he'd suddenly feel like having something to eat, and by now he'd gotten used to the fact that I could always sort something out for him. But no one ever complained. We all knew the revolution would only succeed if each of us, whether a minister or a bodyguard, gave all he had.

And four years of my life flew by like that, years in which a great deal happened in Cuba. Fidel carried out the agrarian reform, thanks to which all the land passed into the possession of the state. He took the factories away from the Americans. He organized campaigns to combat illiteracy, which in Batista's day nobody in Cuba had bothered about.

It all happened so fast that my memory of those years is poor. I didn't even have a home; I slept wherever Fidel happened to be.

Until one day Celia Sánchez, his close friend and companion since the Sierra Maestra days, took me aside and said, "Erasmo, you've got a great talent for cooking! Fidel can have as many bodyguards as he wants, but it's hard to find a reliable chef. Maybe you should get special training?"

It was a great compliment, because Celia had very often cooked for him herself, and Fidel used to say he only liked the food she prepared.

I had already been wondering if the army life was right for me, thinking that in fact I got more pleasure out of cooking, those moments when I could see how the spices totally changed the flavor. How the same dish came out slightly dif-

ferent every time I made it. And above all, how Fidel and all
the others liked what I had cooked.

I told Celia it was a great idea. Yes, I'd like to go to culinary
school.

My fellow guerrillas were amazed. Me? Fidel's bodyguard?
That was the most direct route to becoming an officer.

But I stuck to my guns, and Fidel agreed, and so instead of
being his bodyguard, I became a kitchen boy.

To get into the school, I had to pass a cooking test. I remember that I cooked a fillet of fish in diced mango sauce,
which won me first place. Even I was surprised. For that sauce
you have to have very good demi-glace, which is a thick stock.
You take marrow bones, chop them into small pieces, and
bake them for twenty minutes in an oven set at a very high
temperature. The best sauce comes from ox bones, but in fact
you can use any kind of bones.

Meanwhile, you fry carrots, tomatoes, and celery in olive
oil. Once the bones are browning, you put everything in a large
pot and simmer it over a very low flame. For how long? At least
two days. A well-made demi-glace has the consistency of aspic.
The rest of it is simple: you fillet the fish and fry it, ideally in
olive oil. In a separate pot you heat up the demi-glace. Once
it's hot and the fish is cooked, you add the mango, but wait
until the last minute, because it disintegrates very quickly. The
mango should be diced, not too small and not too big, about
the size of a thumbnail. You cook it until the mango starts to
dissolve. Once the fillet is fried, you pour the sauce over it.

Later I used to cook that dish for Fidel, who liked it very
much. I knew the recipe from a restaurant in Santa Clara.

The school was wonderful. We had teachers from France,

Italy, and Paraguay. Surprisingly, there was no one from the Soviet Union, though the island had been full of Russians ever since the Americans had placed an embargo on Cuba. My favorite teacher was a man named David Griego who had been a chef at an expensive hotel, the Habana Libre. To be a good cook—especially one who cooks for such prominent people—it's not enough to know how to cook. Anyone can learn to do that; if you have a recipe and you make it once or twice, it can't fail to come out well. But if you work in the president's kitchen, you have to be able to plan the work well and to delegate the tasks properly. You have to plan several hours, sometimes even days ahead. I'd had no way of learning how to do that as a bodyguard. And that's the knowledge David Griego passed on to me.

One day, after about a year of school, Celia asked me to come and see her. She complained that Fidel often forgot to eat all day. Or someone would cook for him, but he'd say he didn't like the food and then start making himself spaghetti in the middle of the night; that was one of the things nobody else could cook for him, not even Celia.

So Celia asked if I could sometimes come by after school to cook for him.

Of course I agreed.

7.

He always loved good alcohol and cigars. In May 1958, when Batista's offensive began, he wrote a desperate letter to Celia Sánchez from the Sierra Maestra: "I have no tobacco, I have no wine, I have nothing. A bottle of rosé wine, sweet and Spanish, was left ... in the refrigerator. Where is it?"*

"Of course he liked good alcohol," confirms Erasmo, when I read him that quotation. "But who doesn't? And Fidel ate the same things as the average Cuban."

"Really?" I say doubtfully, because the vision of Fidel as everyone's pal who eats exactly the same food as the common people has too strong an odor of propaganda. "The average Cuban stood in line for hours to buy a rotten tomato. No one was allowed to catch a single fish without state permission. Did Fidel really eat only a little better than they did?"

Erasmo frowns.

"The lines were thanks to the Americans and their embargo; they weren't Fidel's fault," he hisses. "And his meals weren't all that different from the people's."

"Seriously?" I ask again. "So did he eat steaks made of grapefruit? Did he drink sugar water for his dinner, like many a Cuban when the Soviet Union collapsed?"

"What do you know about it?"

Erasmo angrily tosses a dishcloth on the table. He turns away in a sulk and starts pointedly typing on his phone.

And I'm afraid I've gone too far. I'm worried there are things he might not tell me; at the time of our conversations, Fidel is still alive, and his brother Raúl is president. I have to drop it. So to smooth things over, in a conciliatory tone I ask, "Does Fidel actually have any faults?"

Erasmo considers this question for quite a while.

"One," he says at last. "He always knows best."

---

* Tad Szulc, *Fidel: A Critical Portrait* (Perennial, 2002), 86.

All the biographies of Castro confirm this. At every step of the way *el Comandante* lectured everyone else on every conceivable topic. He was sure he knew best about baseball, politics, irrigation, cultivating rice, making cheese, history, geography, fishing, and everything else.

"His famous speeches that went on for hours were the result of this conviction," explains my pal Miguel. "He really did think he knew everything best. And that no one could explain better how to build a communist society, or how to inseminate heifers."

He was already like that as a student. One day he went to see one of his professors. Almost as soon as he entered the house he was lecturing the maid on how to fry plantains.

As president he often ate at the Habana Libre, the best hotel in town. There he explained to the chefs how to cook lobster, how to make duck confit, and how exactly to prepare red snapper, known in Cuba as *pargo rojo*. This hotel, which before the revolution belonged to the Hilton chain, has always employed the very best chefs. But even they had to listen patiently to Fidel's tirades.

Fidel's own recipe for lobster and shrimp features in his interview with the Dominican friar Frei Betto: "The best thing is not to boil either shrimp or lobster, because boiling water reduces the substance and the taste and toughens the flesh. I prefer to bake or broil them. Five minutes of broiling is enough for shrimp. The lobster takes 11 minutes to bake or six minutes on a skewer over hot coals. Baste only with butter, garlic, and lemon. Good food is simple food."[*]

Fidel loved to prepare lobster and red snapper himself. He often devoted himself to this task during his famous fishing expeditions,

---

[*] Frei Betto, *Fidel and Religion: Conversations with Frei Betto on Marxism and Liberation Theology*, trans. Mary Todd (Ocean Press, 2006), 29.

when there was soup made of turtles bred for him right next to his residence at Cayo Piedra. Later, he would stand by the barbecue and personally cook meat for his guests.

It was a gesture of the highest respect to be served fish prepared by Fidel.

8.

Flores

. . . If you must know, it was my brother who taught me to cook; he worked at a restaurant and when he came home he showed me how to split a crayfish in half, how to season shrimp, before that I didn't know anything else except yams, manioc, and the meat that was available in the countryside—chicken, beef, or pork, and also guavas, corn, fried plantains, oranges, beans, and a few hundred pesos I get as my pension is entirely enough for me, a man hasn't got two stomachs, you're not gonna eat two pieces of chicken or two loaves of bread, and as for alcohol I drink . . .

. . . I only drink a drop, look, I pour a little rum into a glass, I add water, and I pour coffee on top, I like that a lot, then I sit in my chair, look, right here, close my eyes a while, and then for a while I can stop thinking about all sorts of things, because I've got all kinds of thoughts in my head, and sometimes I feel as if those thoughts are trying to run off, out of my head, and I don't know what to do, I just sit and try to get a grip on them, sometimes I don't even bother to try, and sometimes I manage to focus on one of them, sometimes I fail.

What else? My wife?

... My wife ...

... my wife and I lived in harmony, we have two children, a son and a daughter, but ...

... but when my father's family refused to agree to him marrying my mother, one night my father took one of his father's horses and rode to my mother's house, where she was already waiting for him—she told her parents she was going for a walk in the garden—my father rode up, she got on the horse, and they ran away toward the village, where my father had rented a house, and where from that day they lived together; my father even sent the horse back to his father, because he said that as his family was standing in his way, as they refused to agree to his marriage to the girl he had chosen, he didn't want a single centavo from a family like that, or any land (though my grandfather had a lot of it), nor a single animal, and for many years he didn't speak to them, although my grandma wrote letters, but the most important thing of all, my dear ...

... the most important thing of all is who throws the ball first, baseball isn't just about muscle power, it's also about knowing how to scare your opponent, and if the first pitcher does his job well, that can decide the whole game, because the other team loses heart and is bewildered; it's just the same in politics, if we let the Americans throw the ball first, something gets turned upside down here—their pitcher will strike us out before he's even thrown the ball, and you have to ask why they didn't come here when we were poor, when the Soviet Union collapsed and the Russians left our country just about overnight, and in just a few months almost all our pigs died, I was there, I drove around with a vet who tried to save at least a few farms, and I went with him because we didn't have enough meat, not even for Fidel, and the vet checked to see if the famine had reached them yet, and I remember how at farm after farm he threw up his hands in despair because it was impossible, it was impossible to save a single one of the farms we visited, so why didn't they come then, why are they coming now, when we're picking ourselves up and our peso is the strongest it has ever been? Can you answer that for me, boy? . . .

. . . but *el Comandante*, if you must know, had eggs for breakfast every day, best of all were quail's eggs, that was a modest meal, with some beans and a little rice, and one time . . .

. . . one time he was sitting at the Hotel Nacional with Comrade Che, just the two of them, Fidel and Che, and the waiter brought them ice cream, *el Comandante* loved ice cream, he could eat ten scoops or more with his dinner, but that time his hands were shaking badly, the waiter's of course, and *el Comandante* said to that waiter, "My friend, you try the ice cream first," and the waiter went completely white in the face, and that was the first time they thought they should really have someone to test what they ate, but my father . . .

. . . my father taught me one thing: you heard nothing— look, watch what's going on, draw conclusions, but keep your ears blocked, and when as a little kid I worked as a shoeshine boy, I stuck to that advice, my daddy said keep your ears closed, people will talk about all sorts of things, but if you don't want trouble, forget it all right away, and for shining shoes, I can still remember, I got five centavos a pair, that's why . . .

... that's why these days I can't live with people, I can't get used to the fact that while I go to church, board the bus, buy a newspaper, read the Bible, and say my prayers, the young people have no respect at all for the old ones, I pay one peso for the bus, but does anyone offer an old person their seat? No, everyone looks right through the old people these days ...

... and yet *el Comandante* once said that when a black man becomes president of the United States, maybe that will be an opportunity to start talking to the Americans, but it didn't look as if it would ever happen. And if now *el Comandante* hasn't met with President Barack Obama, it's because he doesn't want to, not because the president of the United States has something to say here; nobody's gonna dictate to Fidel, and he understands that in baseball the most important thing is who throws the first ball, *el Comandante* is the best at baseball, and if anyone's gonna throw the first ball, he is, and yet ...

... and yet you have to remember that once Fidel told me he'd eat elver salad, they're long and thin, like pieces of spaghetti; he said he'd tried that salad once so I should find him some elvers and learn how to prepare them, and he smiled because it was a known fact, he knew me well enough to be sure I'd find him those elvers, even if I had to get into the water and catch them with my own teeth, so his bodyguard and I went to the fishermen and asked who might have elvers, we drove like that almost all night, until we found this one guy who said he knew a place where you could catch them, but that it was forbidden, so I told him, "Fuck you, man, you're taking us there right now to get those motherfucking elvers," and right away he understood he was talking to someone important, because I spoke to him so firmly, so we got into his boat, sailed off, and in the morning, after a night without sleep, I added lettuce, tomatoes, oregano, chopped parsley, onion, and carrots to the elvers, so he got his elvers, he knew, he knew for sure he could always count on me, he ate it and smiled, but he didn't say a word, he didn't have to say anything, he only had to look at me. I could see by the look in his eyes that everything was okay . . .

. . . look out, look out, look out, look out the window, see that, the tree, the mango tree, a very fine fruit . . .

. . . I wondered how to get down without bruising it . . .

. . . there's a lime tree growing next to it, and the bushes below are tomatoes, we plant them here in Havana by the houses or in the yards outside the apartment blocks, because it can be hard to buy them sometimes, and if I have my own, I'm not dependent on no one, I don't have to get on the bus and go to the *mercado*, I don't have to ask anyone for anything, I just have my own tomatoes whenever I want, I just go outside and pick myself one or two, but then . . .

. . . but then I love *el Comandante* as if he were my father, as if he were my brother; if he came here today and said, "Flores, I need your hand," I'd cut off my hand and give it to him; if he said, "Flores, I need your heart," I'd give him my heart . . .

. . . once I sailed with him to a coral reef, it was a beautiful, sunny day and he went diving, there were always two bodyguards with him who had the same blood type as he did in case anything were to happen, so . . .

. . . so those comrades took the mango from me, I picked a few more too, as I was up the tree, and they drove on, and that was when I joined the revolution and furtively started painting slogans on the walls: "Viva el 26 de Julio," and when Batista's police came and asked who'd done it, I said, "But I don't know how to read and write, I don't even know what it means, and they left me alone."

That's all I can say. I can't say more. Truly, believe me. I'd like to, but I can't. Because they'll come. I'd rather they didn't come.

. . . though I'll tell you one more thing, I'll tell you I prefer animals to people, take my dog, for example; he wandered up to me in the street, he refused to leave me alone, so I took him, cooked him some rice, and he ate until he was fit to burst, and ever since he's been sitting on the doormat, and as soon as I go anywhere, he runs after me; I've given him the name Beethoven, because if something doesn't suit him he pretends he can't hear, Beethoven, come here, Beethoven! You see, he's doing it again, he doesn't want to come so he'll pretend it's not him I'm calling, and yet . . .

. . . and yet when *el Comandante* has a free moment he sails his boat to the reef and dives, but none of his bodyguards can even dream of diving as deep or of catching as fine a fish, as fine a crayfish as he can; then they come back from the trip with a whole sack full of fish, I've seen it many times, and everything they have was caught by *el Comandante*; then I split the crayfish this way, in half, down the middle, we toss the meat on the barbecue, pour on lime juice, and that kind of food, the simplest, is what Fidel likes the best, I know for sure, I made it for him only yesterday, though sometimes . . .

. . . though sometimes my heart wakes me; then I sit up in bed and wait for it to calm down, and if it does, I go back to sleep, but if it doesn't, I wait until the sun rises and I go out of the house to stop thinking about things, because if I start to think I've got all kinds of thoughts in my head, maybe I should write them down, that's what my ex-wife once told me, write it down, Flores, all the stuff that's going around in your head, write it down, or else it'll be bad for you, that's what she said, and I tried to do it, but when I wake up at night, it's still dark, often there's no light, so before the sun shows its face, often there are already so many thoughts going through my head that I don't know which one I should write down, and my wife?

... My wife ...

... my wife left.

... she preferred to live apart instead of with me, and when I go to her and try to explain that those thoughts aren't because of me, that's just the way I am, there's just something happening to me, she drives me away, so then I think about the mango, yes ...

... it really was a very fine fruit and I wondered how to climb down the tree without bruising it, and there was a column of army cars coming along below.

9.

My interpreter and guide Jorge spends almost two weeks with me. Together we go and see everyone who has ever had anything to do with Fidel's dinner table. Among others, Jorge takes me to see his teacher from a bartender's course, who for many years was Fidel's personal waiter. We visit him at his home in a residential district of Havana.

"Fidel? One time he was eating a piece of chicken and choked on it really badly," recalls the former waiter. "He got a bone stuck in his throat. We watched dumbstruck for three or four seconds; we stared at the bodyguards, and they stared at us, and meanwhile he was choking. I was the first to come to my senses. I raced up and clapped him on the back with all my strength. That did the trick, and he started to breathe again, so you could say I saved his life. Plenty of people in Cuba would gladly hang me for that," he says, laughing.

We have to interrupt our work only once. One day at about noon, his boss summons Jorge urgently to the restaurant. That evening my Cuban friend is the assistant waiter serving Barack Obama and his wife, daughters, and mother-in-law, who have come to dine at his restaurant.

"The president had sirloin steak, and the First Lady had steak in wine sauce," Jorge informs me when we meet late that night. "But the most extraordinary thing occurred just after dinner. President Obama looked me in the eyes and said, 'Jorge, that was a great pleasure.'"

"What did you like so much about that?" I ask.

"He remembered my name!" says Jorge. "Can you imagine? Sometimes Cuban politicians come to our place, and there's no question of any of them saying a single friendly word to me. And here's the president of a superpower looking me in the eye and talking to me by name. I'll never forget that moment to the day I die!"

The next day Erasmo hugs Jorge, as if the young man had gone through a baptism by fire.

"Now you know what it's like to work for a president," he says.

10.

Erasmo

The biggest problem with Fidel was that with the guerrillas he had learned to eat at various times of day. It was impossible to plan ahead with him. For a cook that's a tricky situation. You're on the job at any time of the day or night.

But I was also aware of the pluses. Fidel wasn't the type to complain; he ate what I made for him. If anyone was going to criticize the cook, it was more likely to be Raúl.

One time we went to Birán, where Fidel was raised and where his mother lived to the end of her life; his father died before the revolution. They had an enormous farm there. Fidel had eight siblings, and if they had stayed on their father's farm, each of them would have had a very good life. But he brought about the revolution, and he had to set an example. When he carried out the agrarian reform, one of the first farms in Cuba that he took into state ownership was his father's. He left his mother with nothing but a small cottage.

His father had earned it all through hard work. He was no American capitalist of the kind we were to fight against, but a Spaniard from Galicia, who had ended up in Cuba when he was very poor; everything he owned, he had built from scratch. But Fidel couldn't take the land from everyone else and let his mother keep theirs. While he was still fighting in the Sierra Maestra, when he set fire to the large sugarcane plantations, one of the first ones he gave orders to burn down was his father's. Have you ever seen a sugarcane plantation on fire? I have. It leaves a sticky, sugary taste in the air.

His mother never forgave him for that. Of course she was very pleased when he came to visit and always received us cordially—I think she loved him the best of all her children—but it was plain to see there was ill feeling between them. They only ever talked about very general topics: "How's life?" "Everything's fine"; "lots of work"; "it's hot today." Our other comrades and I often offered to leave them alone, but Fidel didn't like being left on his own with his mother. "There's no need," he'd say.

His father had regarded him as a troublemaker who'd never amount to anything in life. He could have expanded the family estate. He was very capable: he'd graduated from high school and then law school with top grades. He could have become anyone he liked. A politician? Any party would have chosen him as its leader. An athlete? The American baseball league offered him a professional contract. A chef? He was a great cook, and if he'd gone to the same school as I did, I'm sure he'd have become the best chef in all of Cuba.

But he earned a law degree and started to help the poor, instead of opening a legal practice for the rich. He could hardly make ends meet.

His mother was a superb cook. Before she became old Castro's second wife, she'd been his maid, and probably his cook too. I remember one time she cooked paella for us all. I thought I managed very well with the cooking, but I didn't know how to make such a good paella. I tried asking her how she did it, but she just smiled. Good cooks never betray their secrets; they'd rather take them to the grave. I thought she must have added a spice to that dish that I couldn't identify.

Afterward I talked about it with my teacher at culinary school, and he said that in such cases it's often the water that's the critical factor. It may not have a flavor, but its quality can have a tremendous effect on the taste of the dish. Indeed, quite near the house they had their own spring, and the water from it tasted very good. Maybe there was something to that.

11.

My friend Miguel's father often went to see Fidel and ate food at his place on many occasions.

"If he were still alive, he could tell you some good stories," says Miguel. "For instance, he said Fidel hardly ate a thing at those receptions, but he never stopped talking. And his favorite foods were milk and cheese. Once he succeeded in breeding a record-breaking cow and made all the party members go to his farm to see her. My father went too, though he thought it rather absurd for everyone to waste their time looking at cows instead of working."

In her day, this cow was one of the symbols of the Cuban Revolution. She was mild-natured and had a large, plump udder. That's where she got her name: Ubre Blanca, meaning "White Udder." In Cuba they sang songs about her, they wrote poems, and *Granma*—named for the famous yacht, it was the Cuban equivalent of *Pravda*, the communist propaganda newspaper—regularly reported on how many liters of milk she had produced that day.

Twenty-five years later, the Cuban director Enrique Colina made a documentary movie about the cow.* "Sometimes she didn't want ordinary grass, and we had to look for Bermuda grass or fetch her oranges or grapefruits," said one of the farmhands. "She had a huge udder. She produced more than one hundred liters a day," added another.

A hundred liters. Four times more than the average cow.

Fidel really did love cows and all dairy products—including cheese, ice cream, and pure white milk. In his view the Cubans, as citizens of a country where thousands of cows were made into steaks, didn't eat enough dairy products; before the revolution, fresh milk or yogurt could be bought only in the bigger cities, and people in the countryside were not in the habit of consuming them, nor did they make cheese. For *el Comandante*, teaching them that both the former and the latter were healthy and nutritious was an aim as important as the revolution itself.

Or to put it another way, the revolution had a new battlefront—the kitchen.

This new breed—Fidel's personal invention—was to be called the tropical Holstein. Whenever he could, Castro went in person to the breeding farm and lectured the experts working there—on how to feed the animals, how to treat them, and how to milk them. He even taught them how the cows should be inseminated. But for the first few years the results of the breeding program were very poor.

Until she appeared. Ubre Blanca.

"Apparently, he spotted her when she was still a heifer," says Miguel. "My father told me that Fidel noticed her udder right away and gave orders for her to be kept under close watch, and from then

---

* Enrique Colina, *La vaca de mármol* [The marble cow] (2013), a Cuban-French co-production.

on he was always asking questions about her. And because one of Fidel's nicknames was *El Toro*—the Bull—his love of cows prompted a good deal of hilarity among his comrades in Havana."

When it turned out that Ubre Blanca really was growing into a record breaker, a team of about fifteen people was assembled who were exclusively responsible for her. They brought her special food. They played her classical music to make her feel relaxed during her four daily milking sessions.

Soon after, Ubre Blanca started to break all sorts of records. She was even entered in *The Guinness Book of Records* as the world's most productive dairy cow. The previous record holder was an American cow, which added spice to the milk-yield war.

"Fidel talked about it nonstop, day and night," says Erasmo. "He'd say, 'Five thousand cows like that one will be enough to supply all of Cuba with milk.'"

Ubre Blanca was treated with the kind of great care usually reserved for the most important party dignitaries. Soldiers guarded her around the clock. She also had her own food tasters; the grass or fruit destined for her was first eaten by other animals and only then served to Ubre Blanca.

The scientists were given orders to reproduce the record-breaking cow, but none of her offspring achieved the same level of milk production. Ubre Blanca must have had a sense of the great responsibility that lay with her, because she began to decline. After her third birth she became seriously ill and stopped producing record amounts of milk. What was *Granma* to write about, when it had accustomed its readers to regular reports on the heroic cow's milking sessions? People expected her to be very healthy and breaking new records.

A cow that produced less milk wasn't helping the revolution.

Worse than that, a cow that wasn't producing milk could serve the imperialists as proof that the revolution had stalled.

Cuba didn't need a sick Ubre Blanca. In 1985, Fidel made the decision himself to have her euthanized.

12.

Erasmo

You ask what Fidel used to eat apart from dairy products. Well, he didn't eat much meat, but he loved vegetables, of any kind. And if he did eat meat, what he liked best was mutton, with honey or in coconut milk. How do you make it? You put the lamb in a pot, then add onions, garlic, beans, a little black pepper, and a bay leaf, and you pour wine on top. It doesn't matter what kind, but white is best. You can also add a glass of brandy. You cook it all together for half an hour.

Then you have to heat up your demi-glace. While it's cooking, you add a pinch of nutmeg. Once the meat is cooked, you strain off the sauce and add coconut milk. Finally, you season it with a pinch of salt and some cilantro.

He also liked *lechón asado*, suckling pig, an animal that has been fed only on its mother's milk. You gut the piglet, but you leave the skin, head, and tail. Then you marinate it for twenty-four hours in a *mojo criollo* sauce: to make this, you squeeze orange juice and add a drop of olive oil, chopped parsley, crushed garlic, and of course some demi-glace. You press the meat in a special gridiron to roast well on all sides, and you steep it in the sauce.

For the first hour you roast it at a temperature of 150 degrees (300 degrees Fahrenheit), and for the second at 180 degrees (360 degrees Fahrenheit). Then you open the oven and baste the piglet's skin with lard to make it brown well. Fidel liked to eat it with baked plantains.

If he'd gone on a trip, sometimes he'd call me before starting out on the return journey to say, "Surprise me today, Erasmo."

So I had to surprise him. Though it wasn't at all easy; after all, we'd known each other for decades.

13.

Julia Jimenez, a forty-five-year-old doctor in jeans with fashionable holes in them, has been living in Orlando, Florida, for twenty-five years. She was still a teenager when, like thousands of other Cubans, she and her parents escaped across the sea. I'm meeting her while staying the night at a small hotel run by her aunt in Matanzas; I want to see what people eat in the Cuban provinces, and I've heard that at this hotel they feed you very well. Julia has come to visit her aunt for the first time since her escape to the United States. Each day we sit together on the fabulously colorful colonial patio, while Julia's aunt, Doña Juanita, a small, bony old woman who never stops smiling, brings us all sorts of delicious food for breakfast, lunch, and dinner.

As I gush with praise for the beef, lobster, and steaks marinated in orange juice, known here as a *palomilla* steak, that she has prepared, Julia says confidentially, "My aunt is from Nitza's school."

And when I ask who Nitza is, Julia smiles broadly and explains, "Everything that's best about Cuban cuisine. And everything that's worst too."

Then she says her aunt will tell me better, so she calls Doña Juanita over to our table. The old woman sits down and spreads her skirt between her legs, and I'm all ears as, from behind a steaming bowl of soup, I listen to the story of Nitza.

Nitza Villapol became a phenomenon in the 1950s, when television first reached Cuba. She appeared on it once a week, to teach the Cuban housewives the right way to cook steak and how to make a sophisticated dessert. Along the way, as happens on TV, she advertised American blenders, toasters, and other kitchen appliances. And she wrote cookbooks, which to this day are still revered by many Cuban housewives as their kitchen bibles.

"I was thirteen years old then," says Doña Juanita. "We didn't have a TV set, but Nitza's recipes got through to us anyway. People who had televisions used to write them down. Once a week I went to the neighbors' house to copy them out for my mom. I still have them, and I still use them."

Doña Juanita summons her granddaughter. A few minutes later the little girl brings a yellowing notebook from the old dresser. And in it, among other things recorded in beautiful handwriting, we read,

Vaca frita—"fried cow," which is beef with onions;
Ropa vieja—"old clothes," which is meat and vegetables.

After Fidel had seized power, one might have thought Nitza's bourgeois show didn't have a chance of remaining on TV. But the country's new leader appreciated her talents. Nitza went on working, but under new conditions. When the Americans imposed their economic blockade on Cuba, many products disappeared from the stores. In the early 1960s ration cards were introduced, and most people spent several hours a day trying to pull together something to eat. Now Nitza's job was to help them through these tough times.

"I didn't have the slightest idea what the revolution was. I had no personal connection to it," she said many years later. "It was common to see grown men and women going through trash cans foraging for something to eat. When many people were hungry, the rich in Cienfuegos used to have lobster and jumbo shrimp and rich coffee."*

Nitza was happy to take on the mission of cooking for the revolution. Because there was almost nothing to buy in the stores except potatoes, she'd teach people various ways of preparing them: one day she'd make mash with olive oil, the next with onion, and the next with garlic. She'd also instruct them how to make a garnish using lard and orange juice.

It all changed in 1991 with the collapse of the Soviet Union, which until then had sponsored Fidel and his revolutionary experiments. The cash flow from Moscow ceased almost overnight, and it soon became apparent that the island couldn't manage without it.

Fidel called this time the Special Period. A few years earlier there had been a popular joke in Havana that said the signs reading "Don't feed the animals" at the city zoo had been replaced by signs saying "Don't steal the animals' food."

After the collapse of the Soviet Union, people started telling a

---

* Tom Miller, *Trading with the Enemy: A Yankee Travels Through Castro's Cuba* (Basic Books, 2008), 134.

new joke, which said that the signs at the zoo now read "Don't eat the animals."

Another joke went, "What are the three achievements of the Cuban Revolution? Medicine, education, and athletes. And its three failures? Breakfast, lunch, and dinner."

Nitza, too, cooked more and more modestly. She tried some daring culinary experiments, advising the viewers to replace meat with . . . fruit. To this day the Cubans remember her recipe for steak made from grapefruit; you have to fry it in batter, with garlic, and coat it in lime juice. They also say how she taught them to make *ropa vieja*—the famous Cuban dish of shredded beef and vegetables—but recommended substituting plantain peel for the meat.

"It was all wretched," says Doña Juanita pensively. "Especially during the Special Period, when there weren't even any grapefruits. Or limes. Or garlic. Or plantains."

"What did you eat then?" I ask.

But Doña Juanita can't answer. Only from books do I learn that fifty thousand Cubans lost their sight during the Special Period. Every third day, instead of eating, people drank sugar water. They stopped traveling by cab and bus.*

Julia Jimenez grows pensive when we talk about the 1990s.

"We all went hungry. I lost twenty-six pounds during the Special Period, fifteen in just the first year after the fall of the Soviet Union. That was when my father made the decision that we weren't going to wait any longer to see what Fidel would think up next but that we had to leave for America."

---

* For more on this topic, see Philip Brenner and Marguerite Rose Jiménez, eds., *A Contemporary Cuba Reader: Reinventing the Revolution* (Rowman & Littlefield, 2007).

For survival, there was a mass effort to dig vegetable beds next to people's houses, near apartment blocks, in school gardens, and even on balconies. There they planted anything that would grow in Cuba: eggplants, tomatoes, onions, cabbages, zucchini, and cucumbers. They also planted trees that in time began to produce oranges, mangoes, and bananas. To this day, almost every apartment block in Havana has a few vegetable patches in the yard.

"In those days we watched Nitza out of sheer perversity: What will she come up with this time to save the revolution? What will she tell us to eat?" says Doña Juanita.

Nitza, too, lost weight. She battled on for a few more years but spoke with ever dwindling conviction. Until one day, without warning, her show was taken off the air.

14.

Erasmo

Sometimes Americans come here because someone has told them this restaurant belongs to Castro's chef, and they fire questions at me. They ask what he used to eat, and aren't I ashamed to have cooked for him? But those are state secrets. I'm not going to tell just anyone who walks in here off the street about that! With you it's different; you're a friend from Poland. A Pole's going to understand a Cuban quicker than an American: for many years we belonged to the same bloc of states.

And I have no reason to be ashamed. No one ever did as much good for Cuba as Fidel.

The Americans are extremely belligerent, but the most belligerent of all are the Cubans who escaped, settled in the United States, and have come back now to visit the old country. Fall into the hands of one of those guys—God forbid! In the past I used to argue with them, but now I just hide in the kitchen. Every reproach they'd like to hurl at Fidel they hurl at me. How much of that can you listen to? "It was what it was, and now it's different," I'd say, when I was still talking to them. "You couldn't come here, but now you can. Everyone makes choices in life, and everyone pays for them." And I used to add, "What'll happen if you have a heart attack in the middle of the street in the United States? First they'll ask if you've paid for insurance; only then will they save you. If you don't have insurance, they can leave you there to die. Here in Cuba everyone gets medical care."

Did any of it get through to them? I doubt it.

You can criticize Fidel for various things, but there was no falsehood in what he did. "He took away your land?" I always asked them. "He took his own family's land away too. He forced you to leave? No, he didn't. He said that if you want to leave, the door is open, because he was building a country where you weren't going to eat lobster for supper every day."

What's that, Witold? You say now I serve lobster for supper every day at my restaurant? Better leave it at that. Come on, let's go to the kitchen; let's make something else. Put on an apron; grab a knife.

I'll tell you a secret. After Fidel retired, he often called to ask me to come and make him vegetable soup. You can usually tell who's a good cook by their vegetable soup. You can use the same vegetables, in the same proportions, fry the onions for the same length of time, and make a broth using the same chicken and pork—and mine would come out well enough for Fidel to want a second helping, while someone else's would prompt him to complain. Fidel would say to me, "I don't know how you do it, but the food you make is the best."

The recipe? I'm sorry, but I've told you too much already. Like Fidel's mother and her paella recipe, I'll be taking Erasmo's recipe for vegetable soup to the grave.

But perhaps we can make ceviche together. All right? You take a fillet of fish, any kind, as long as the flesh is white. Dice it. Add lemon juice, a drop of olive oil, salt, and pepper. You must also cook some onion to give the dish a strong flavor and aroma. You add one clove of crushed garlic, a little chili, you let it stand in the fridge for fifteen minutes—and it's done.

15.

Flores

... What did you say? ...

... Say it again ...

... Aaaaaaaaa ...

... So you're saying I look like *el Comandante* Fidel Castro? Thank you for saying that, let me shake your hand, or better yet, give me a high five, give me a *choca cinco* as we say, in fact lots of people tell me that and every time it pleases me, I was like him when I was younger too, when he was in a good mood even *el Comandante* sometimes used to say to me, "Flores, you're so similar to me; you could put on my uniform and substitute for me for a few days while I have a rest," but I'd always reply, "*El Comandante*, that's impossible, nobody can replace Fidel," and *el Comandante* was always pleased with that answer, so . . .

. . . so you see, my money ran out, I had to ask my neighbor to give me a cigarette; she gave me two, she's a good neighbor, sometimes she gives me food too, oh, look what I have in the pot, chicken and rice, that's all from her, if you want, take a spoon and have a bite, my ration cards are at her place too, I say to her, "Take it all, salt, beans, chicken, if I need anything, you'll give it to me," but I know she gives me more than there is in those cards. The Cubans are good people, they share with others . . .

. . . and if they don't share . . . well, one time Che was visiting a factory, the manager invited him into his office and said, "*Comandante*, maybe you'd like a cold beer?" and it was really hard to buy beer in Cuba in those days, so Che asks him, "You've got beer for me, but what about my comrades?" to which the manager says, "I haven't enough beer for them, but I can offer them cold water." And you know what? Right away he stopped being the manager. Che said to him, "What sort of a communist are you if you only have beer for me?"

. . . that's all I can say . . .

. . . really, believe me, I can't say more. I'd rather they didn't come here . . .

. . . though I will tell you one more thing, namely I'll tell you that Fidel loves ice cream, he can eat fifteen scoops, he can eat twenty, he always wanted every Cuban to be able to buy ice cream every day, every Cuban to be able to go to Coppelia,*

---

* A legendary ice cream parlor in Havana.

and for there to be more flavors there than at any ice cream parlor in the United States; he had them make ice cream out of sheep's milk, donkey's milk, he even had them make ice cream out of bison's milk, and when he tried them, he said they were really good, and they should make them more often . . .

. . . but then you can't eat two pieces of meat, you can't eat two crayfish, not even *el Comandante* when he sails his boat to the reef and dives, and none of his bodyguards can even dream of diving that deep, or of catching a fish or a crayfish as big as he can, out of everything he catches, he eats only one crayfish. Just *one single* crayfish, the rest is shared among the others.

16.

Fidel grew old and ill, but he never stopped thinking about the revolution and its culinary battlefront. In 2005 he announced a major pressure-cooker campaign—every month 100,000 pressure cookers were distributed to households throughout Cuba. In all, the Cubans were given more than 2 million of these pots.

In 2008 he stepped down from power for good, and when some people thought he must have died, he suddenly appeared at a cheese factory. There he gave a talk that lasted several hours about the changing world and about how the Cuban dairy industry should develop.

He died eight months after Barack Obama's visit—and mine—to Havana.

A few days later I call Erasmo to offer my condolences.

"I'm crying like a baby," he says. "I'm actually surprised, because
we all knew how old he was, we knew he couldn't live forever; I
thought I was ready for it. I wasn't. I was with him for almost sixty
years. I kept going to see him until his final days. When he wanted
me to cook something for him, someone from his house would call
me, and I'd come and cook. On the day he died, I was on my way
there, but then I got a call from an old friend from the army days
who was with him to the end. 'Don't come, Erasmo,' he said. 'That's
it?' was all I asked. 'Yes,' he replied, and hung up."

17.

Flores

... But then ...

   ... but then the first time I came to Fidel's house, with a
sack of coal on my back, when I opened the door, he was
standing there, *el Comandante* Fidel Castro, just in his pajamas, watch your head, he said, laughing, and pulled my cap
down over my ears, yes, *Comandante*, I said, I'll watch out, I
threw the sack beside the hearth and started to make a meal,
and *el Comandante* stood next to me and asked if I knew how
to cook turkey, I replied, yes, I do, *el Comandante*, I do, so he
sat next to me, he looked at me, and he asked if I knew how to
cook it without bones, so I replied, yes, I do, *el Comandante*, I
do, and he asked if I'm sure I know how to make it properly,
and without waiting for me to reply, he told me how to bone a
turkey properly, Flores, he said, remember that you always
remove the bones from a turkey through its asshole, and he

started to laugh, and I started to laugh with him, and then *el Comandante* ate the turkey I'd roasted for him, and he didn't say a word, but he didn't have to say anything, because I knew that if he was silent it meant he liked it . . .

. . . That's all I can tell you. I'll always care about him, Fidel, my *Comandante*. He's everything to me. He's my entire life . . .

. . . I saw him only yesterday, standing in the garden, right here, you peek out the window, he was standing there smiling at me, and I looked at him to see if he needed anything, we could always communicate through glances, he only had to blink and I knew I should go up to him, but this time he made it clear I wasn't needed, and that everything was proceeding to plan.

Forgive me, but that's really all I can say. And now you'd better go.

Dessert

បង្អែម

Papaya Salad

The Story of Yong Moeun,
Pol Pot's Chef

1.

First I hear ringing, infectious laughter. It's so alluring that I spontaneously feel like joining in and laughing too, never mind why, or whether it makes sense. I have to keep reminding myself whom I've come to see: Pol Pot. Genocide. The killing fields. And I must mentally replay the movie that's familiar to anyone who has ever taken the slightest interest in Cambodia: the skulls, tibias, pelvic bones, ribs, and spines. Almost two million victims in less than four years.

So first there's laughter, and only then does she appear. Yong Moeun. For many years she cooked for one of the greatest dictators of the twentieth century.

To find her, I've come to Anlong Veng, a town that's strung along the shores of a lake known as Ta Mok—so named in honor of the bloodthirsty last leader of the Khmer Rouge, or rather the grave digger for what was left of them.

The houses here, as throughout the rest of Cambodia, have been built quickly, without a plan, and—often—chaotically, carelessly. Among them, like industrious beetles in a rotting palm tree, former

Khmer Rouge soldiers are bustling about, and so are their children or grandchildren. Anlong Veng was their final enclave. This is where the greatest diehards, the ones who believed in the revolution to the bitter end, finished up.

Pol Pot died in the jungle that surrounds the town in 1998. His remaining soldiers went on defending themselves for another year, until Ta Mok was arrested and taken by helicopter to a prison in Phnom Penh.

First I have to drive around an absurd monument—a dove standing on a white sphere guarded by four deer—that's supposed to symbolize peace. Then I pass a small restaurant and a stream pouring into a lake, before seeing a gas station, and behind it, some large tamarind roots drying on the porch. Yong Moeun greets me with a firm handshake and a laugh. I haven't said a word yet, and already she's laughing.

So I remind myself once again: Pol Pot, with Pol Pot, about Pol Pot, for Pol Pot, because of Pol Pot.

But it's no good. Auntie Moeun's laughter is as infectious as polio. I shake her hand and begin to laugh with her.

2.

I married too early. That's what I think now.

My husband's name was Pich Cheang—look, here's his picture. He went to the same school as I did and knew my brother, and he said I'd caught his eye much earlier on.

But only when he found out that I belonged to the Organization too did he regard me as the perfect candidate for a wife. So he went to ask my brother if he'd agree to our marriage.

My brother started telling me how clever and brave Pich Cheang was. He really was clever: he'd graduated from school with distinction and was one of the best students they'd ever had. He wasn't short of courage either; not without reason was he made a general many years later.

Except that I didn't really know which one of my brother's friends he was. But I was already committed to the revolution, and Koy Thuon had convinced me that communists should intermarry. We met, and we talked. Pich Cheang made a very good impression on me. "Well, why not?" I thought.

At the time, my future husband was working at a rubber factory, officially as an ordinary laborer. In fact he had gotten a job there to encourage people to join us. He already had a wide network when the government soldiers got wind of what he was doing. Luckily, someone warned him in time. From then on, Pich Cheang went into hiding, so we married in secret. We drove out of town to the home of one of our friends. Our school friends came, and also some workers from the rubber factory who had been enlisted into the party by my husband. Koy Thuon solemnly announced, in the name of Angkar, that we were husband and wife. Then everyone dispersed so the army wouldn't catch us holding a gathering.

The party rented us a small house in a village in Kratié province. It was a friendly village; all its inhabitants supported us. One day a woman appeared there too. Pich Cheang didn't say who she was. Maybe he didn't know; I didn't ask questions. "Sister Ponnary" was how he introduced her. She wasn't pretty, but her hands were very soft; you could tell she had never worked in the fields or at the cooking pots.

I didn't ask where she was from. Or who was after her,

because she was obviously running away from the soldiers. I just made sure nobody bothered her. Occasionally, she took me aside and said she dreamed of a Cambodia where every child would be able to go to school.

"That's my dream too," I'd reply, but if I'm going to be frank, she didn't stir sympathy in me. She never said much. She seemed rather superior. So when, a month later, two men appeared and led her away toward the jungle, I sighed with relief that she was finally gone.

Pich Cheang and I had a strange marriage. While he toured the country and organized party cells, I delivered Angkar's messages to other villages and towns. We hardly ever saw each other.

Until one day Pich Cheang was arrested, and for the next three years we didn't see each other at all.

3.

He was a very polite boy who "never caused trouble."[*]

That's how Seng, his older brother, described Pol Pot many years later. And he spoke the truth. Everyone remembers little Saloth Sâr, as the future dictator was really named, as an extremely nice, sweet-natured child.

"He was born in 1925. Cambodia was still a French colony then," says Soeum Borey, a history teacher at one of the schools in Phnom Penh, whom I meet at a trendy café in the city center. "His father

---

[*] Seth Mydans, "Pol Pot's Siblings Remember the Polite Boy and the Killer," *New York Times*, September 6, 1997.

was a wealthy farmer. Pol Pot's sister even became one of the wives of the king of Cambodia."

Pol Pot's brother couldn't understand what had happened to Sâr after he left home.* As an adolescent he was an average student. When he left home to go to school in Phnom Penh, he wasn't interested in politics at all. He played a lot of soccer and a bit of music and was such a poor student that after a few years he had to leave his prestigious high school and instead go to a technical college in the suburbs. But there he caught up with his studies and got a scholarship to go to Paris.

He sailed to France with twenty other scholarship students. Soon they were all missing Khmer food. So at a stopover in Djibouti two of the students bought lemons, pepper, and spices. They brought it all on board the ship to make some Khmer food. Sâr did the cooking.† What exactly did he make? Where had he learned to cook?

Unfortunately, I couldn't find anyone who remembers seeing the young Pol Pot with a wooden spoon in his hand.

4.

Brother, don't think I was the only one who noticed Brother Pouk's smile or saw what a handsome man he was. There were always girls from the village at our base, and lots of them were in love with him. They'd start to giggle whenever he walked past, and although I had a husband, I used to giggle with

---

* Ibid.

† Philip Short, *Pol Pot: The History of a Nightmare* (John Murray, 2006), 45.

them. We were all young, and he was so handsome. Several times we almost wept with laughter.

But Pol Pot took no notice.

I'd been at the base for well over a year when one day, out of the blue, at breakfast, I saw a familiar face. Those same soft hands. That same smile she wore when talking to me about schools and education. "It's Auntie Ponnary," I instantly realized.

Yes, it was her.

"Sister, meet Brother Pouk's wife," someone said.

I was dumbstruck.

Why had nobody ever told me that Brother Pouk had a wife?

I felt sorry that Angkar had to keep even things like that a secret. But I pretended nothing was wrong. I bowed politely and said we'd met before. She smiled and said she remembered me. I served breakfast and then cleared the plates. I didn't utter another word.

From then on Auntie Ponnary was at our base permanently. She lived with Brother Pouk and ate her meals with the other comrades. I got used to her company, especially since in the meantime my husband, Pich Cheang, had gotten out of prison. One day he, too, turned up at the base. I didn't recognize him. He'd always been thin, but now he looked as if someone had just pulled on skin over bones. But he smiled broadly and said, "Hello, Comrade Moeun."

Pol Pot was smiling too. "Sister Moeun is always overfeeding us." He started to laugh, and Pich Cheang laughed with him.

5.

By day he drove a good car, a Citroën, which few people in Cambodia could afford. He worked with the chairman of the Democratic Party, the main opposition force in Cambodia, and dated Soeung Son Maly, one of the most beautiful girls in Phnom Penh. But by night he went to underground meetings where he and others planned the revolution.

"Saloth Sâr returned from his studies in Paris a full-fledged revolutionary," says the historian Soeum Borey. "It was there that he began to spend time in very politically active company. He immersed himself in politics until it became his obsession."

In Paris, Sâr met Ieng Sary and Khieu Samphan. These two men would become his closest comrades for many years. He also joined the Cercle Marxiste, the Marxist circle of communist-leaning students from which would emerge the germ of the Khmer Rouge.

"When he flunked the second year of his studies, the Organization sent him back to Cambodia. The country was in total chaos. The young communists from Paris wanted someone on the ground to find out what organizations were being formed there and which of them had aims similar to their own," Borey explains. "First Sâr was in Phnom Penh; then he went to the headquarters of the Vietcong, which at that time was at war with the United States."

A few years later he came back from the Vietcong base. He renewed his acquaintance with Soeung Son Maly and for a while dated her again. But seeing that Sâr's political career didn't augur well, the girl decided to marry someone else.

"Apparently, Sâr took it very badly," says Soeum Borey. "From then on, the revolution became his whole life."

Soon after the beautiful Soeung's wedding, Sâr, too, got married. His bride was Khieu Ponnary—the sister-in-law of Ieng Sary, his friend from Paris, and the first woman in the history of Cambodia to earn a master's degree.

For several years he worked as a teacher at one of the local high schools. Once again, he left very good memories behind him.

"I once met a teacher from the old days who worked with Pol Pot at the same school for a year," says Soeum Borey. "He said that you rarely come across a teacher who's so obliging and so well liked by the students. It's extraordinary, especially when you think how the Khmer Rouge closed down all the schools."

But Sâr didn't work for long. The Cambodian ruler, Prince Sihanouk, refused to tolerate the Communist Party, and an ever-tighter noose began to close around the group of former Paris students. They decided it was time to transfer the revolution to the jungle. They would come back only when they were ready to fight for total power.

6.

My guide Soeum and I are driving through the Cambodian province. It's sad here; the government has allowed large corporations to cut down almost all the jungle, mainly firms from Thailand that have made money from the timber. Now barren wasteland stretches all the way to a plateau. It'll take the jungle centuries to grow back again, if it ever does.

Soeum asks if I want to see a crater left by an American bomb. The Americans dropped hundreds of thousands of bombs here in the 1960s, but most of the craters have grown over by now or have been filled in. Apparently, this one is still in pretty good shape.

I do want to see it.

So we drive off the surfaced road onto a sandy one, which we slide along for a couple of miles, until we reach a small village where a herd of emaciated but tail-wagging dogs assails us. They bark at us, perhaps more out of a sense of duty than the belief that they're going to scare us away. Soeum goes into one of the bamboo huts. This is the home of Uncle Keo, the oldest person in the village. I'm told he's ninety, and remembers a great deal. In a country where almost half the population is under thirty, his longevity and memory are valuable.

Soeum asks Uncle Keo if he'd show us the crater, and the old man puts on some plastic slippers, picks up a solid stick to lean on, and gets into the car with us.

"I remember when they dropped those bombs," he says, waving his stick to the left to indicate where we have to turn. "The planes that carried the bombs could be heard from a long way off. We were terrified because of the immense damage the bombs could cause. In the next village, one of those bombs fell on a temple and killed twelve people. In ours, the home of a family with eight children was hit."

Uncle Keo points with his stick to tell us to park the car by some gray-and-brown brushwood. We continue on foot.

The crater is just behind the bushes. It's overgrown with grass and scrub, but its size makes quite an impression.

"Immediately after the explosion, you could have put three elephants in it, one standing on top of another," says Uncle Keo. "Now you could still put two in there."

The bombs were dropped on Cambodia under the code name Operation Menu, and each successive act in this crime was named for a meal. The final decision to drop them was made in March 1969, two months after Richard Nixon came to power. The Vietnamese communists, against whom America was waging war at the time, had bases in Cambodia too.

For "Breakfast," about fifty B-52 bombers dropped more than two thousand tons of bombs on suspected Vietnamese communist bases in Kampong Cham. Instead of hitting the Vietcong, most of the bombs fell on civilians.

Then came time for "Lunch"—more bombs.

Then "Snack."

Then "Dinner."

"Supper."

And "Dessert."

Altogether, Operation Menu dropped almost 110,000 tons of bombs on Cambodia. It happened without the knowledge of the American public. Only a few members of the U.S. military, and the president's administration, knew about it.

But that was just the start.

The war in Vietnam had ended, but the bombs continued to fall on Cambodia. Altogether the Americans dropped over half a million tons of bombs on this tiny country—three times more than on Japan throughout World War II, including the two atom bombs.

As a result of these bombings, at least 100,000 Cambodians were killed. Perhaps many more—it's impossible to establish the precise number.

The more American bombs fell on Cambodia, the more people joined the Khmer Rouge. At the start of 1970, they had barely two thousand armed men. Two years later they had more than thirty thousand. They were in control of almost half the country.

The American public was successfully deceived for over four years. The truth about the raids on Cambodia came to light only after Watergate.*

By August 15, 1973, when the U.S. Congress ordered an end to the bombing, the Khmer Rouge forces numbered between forty and fifty thousand and were steadily advancing on the capital.

7.

We drive Uncle Keo back to his bamboo hut. He takes off his slippers and lies down on the floor; he says in this position it's easier for him to get through the middle of the day, when the heat is at its most intense. He gazes at the ceiling, as if trying to count how many flies have settled there.

We talk a while longer. Soeum doesn't hide the fact that we're going to see Pol Pot's cook. Uncle Keo is lost in thought for a while; finally, he says, "In Pol Pot's time my younger brother was the head of our village. I had a wife in those days. She was working in the fields when he came along, and they had a quarrel about something. She gave him a piece of her mind—after all, we were family; it never occurred to her to be afraid of him. That night my brother's people caught her when she was on her way home. They beat her up so badly that she died two days later. Because she should have been obedient, but wasn't."

Neither Soeum nor I know what to say. I stammer that we're

* Mariusz Zawadzki, *"Brudne sprawki Ameryki"* [America's dirty business], *Gazeta Wyborcza*, February 21, 2014.

very sorry. Soeum translates. But Uncle Keo doesn't so much as cast us a glance; he's lost in his memories.

"My brother and his men killed over fifty people like that. Some they beat up; others they just refused to give food. He wasn't a bad fellow; it's very strange that he behaved that way. Until the Vietnamese came and drove out Pol Pot, and then my brother stopped being in charge. A few years later he fell sick with some sort of cancer, and piece by piece his skin fell off. Apparently, even his nose fell off. I don't know if it's true, because he never left the house, but that's what people said. His wife had left him, and his children didn't want to know him. No one from the village brought him so much as a glass of water. I don't know when he died, but afterward no one wanted to bury him."

"So where is he buried?" asks Soeum.

"Where they all are. By the crater."

"By the crater we were at just a quarter of an hour ago?"

Uncle Keo nods to say yes: right there in the bushes where we parked the car.

So we were walking around on a mass grave, where Uncle Keo's wife and his reprobate brother lie, but we didn't know it.

I ask Soeum to ask Uncle Keo why he didn't tell us.

"You asked about the crater." Not for an instant does he shift his gaze from the flies on the ceiling.

8.

The Khmer Rouge leaders often chose cooks to be their wives. Khieu Samphan, the future head of state, married a woman named So Socheat. The first time he saw her was when she brought food for him and other leaders. Many years later Socheat recalled that from then on, Khieu often came to help her in the kitchen. She didn't know what to make of his advances; he was an intellectual who had studied in Paris, and she was just a simple village girl. "He came to help me peel garlic. I could verify his personality," she said.* Evidently, he passed this test of character, because soon after they were married.

Nuon Chea, Brother Number Two, also married a cook, named Ly Kim Seng. When the Khmer Rouge attained power, Brother Chea took great care to set a good example, and for his wife not to hold any high-ranking positions. While he jointly governed Cambodia, she went on making noodles.

Several times Pol Pot suggested to Nuon Chea that he bring his wife with him on foreign trips. No one would hold it against him; Mrs. Ly was a distinguished freedom fighter who had been in the resistance movement for many years. But Nuon Chea preferred to keep her in the kitchen. He didn't want others to think ill of him for trying to secure privileges for his wife.

Even leaders' wives who were educated and hadn't started their revolutionary lives as cooks often had to stand by the oven, including Yun Yat, wife of Son Sen, later the minister of defense, and Khieu Thirith, wife of Ieng Sary, later minister of foreign affairs. Though in time both women also became ministers—the former of education and the latter of social affairs.

So the wives of four of the five most important men in the regime worked in the kitchen. The only one who was never seen with a ladle in her hand was Pol Pot's wife, Khieu Ponnary.

---

* Lauren Crothers, "Wife Portrays Khieu Samphan as the Loving Family Man," *Cambodia Daily*, June 11, 2013.

There's no other country on earth where the world of cooks is so interwoven with the world of politics.

In our guerrilla days there were very few women at the base; most of them were girls from the villages who came to do some cooking or help in the garden. The leaders were still young; they were attracted to girls, but Angkar didn't tolerate love affairs. If you wanted to spend time with a girl, you had to get married.

Pol Pot and me? I know he liked me, very much. He often asked my opinion on various matters, because he knew I would always tell him frankly what I thought. Occasionally, he came to watch me work in the kitchen. Sometimes I had my head down, because I was hulling corn, for instance, and suddenly I'd sense someone watching me. I'd look up and see Brother Pouk. How long had he been there? And why? I don't know. As soon as I raised my head, he always smiled and left.

But I already had a husband. And Brother Pouk had a wife. There was nothing else to say. We were both married to other people, and Angkar was very firm about such matters.

9.

One evening at supper Auntie Ponnary started to behave differently than usual. She said out loud that we must watch out, because the Vietnamese were our enemies and they were lying in wait to annihilate us.

How strange, I thought. The Vietnamese had been helping

us in our struggle. We'd formed an alliance with them. But of course I didn't say a word.

Brother Pouk instantly stopped eating. He wiped his mouth and left the table.

Nobody argued with Auntie Ponnary about it. That struck me, because the brothers usually discussed everything at length. But this time everyone just finished their supper and went to bed.

I couldn't understand it.

From that night on Auntie Ponnary talked about the Vietnamese more and more. Saying they wanted to kill us or that they hated us. That the Khmer and the Vietnamese had always been enemies.

One day, they were conferring at the table, and one of the adjutants brought Pol Pot a glass of water. Auntie Ponnary tore it from his hands and furiously threw it to the floor. "Sâr!" she shouted. "Sâr, you mustn't drink it! It's poisoned!"

Brother Pol Pot asked her to calm down.

"No, Sâr, I won't!" she went on shouting. "He's put poison in the water! The Vietnamese are trying to poison you!"

She looked at him, and he looked at her.

He didn't say a word, but I'll never forget his sorrow. Pol Pot, always cheerful, always smiling, always full of joy, but that day he looked like a manioc bulb that's been ripped from the ground.

As time went on, there were days when Auntie Ponnary behaved normally: she took part in meetings, presented her views logically, and talked to people in the camp about the revolution and about our everyday life.

And there were times when she talked about the Vietnamese. On those days, she was entirely shut in her own world. It must have been terrifying, because she'd tremble, staring at us with eyes that couldn't see, or she'd wake in the middle of the night and start shouting. That they were coming. Or that we must flee. Then she'd shake poor Brother Pol Pot. She'd wake him up and insist he instantly run away with her into the jungle. Or she'd simply howl like an animal. She could be heard all over the base.

Then I understood why Pol Pot had left the room when she started talking about the Vietnamese.

I also realized who was to live in the bamboo hut near mine, which had stood empty until now.

Auntie Ponnary was locked up in it on the days when she talked about the Vietnamese. She ate, drank, and relieved herself in there.

I went on cooking for her, but one of the Khmer Loeu took the food inside the hut and also removed the plates. I heard occasional cursing and shouting. She'd scream abuse at him, though he merely brought the food and let in the girl who cleaned up Auntie Ponnary's poop. No one wanted to go in there; on a bad day, Auntie Ponnary was quite capable of scratching.

Eventually, Auntie Ponnary would stop shouting. The same girl used to go and comb her hair and help her to wash. Then the Khmer Loeu would move away from the door, and Auntie would appear at our base again and start chatting with people, just as if nothing had ever been wrong. She'd also go back to Brother Pol Pot's hut, and they'd live together again.

I didn't like Auntie Ponnary. Not because she was sick, or because her illness made her shout and be incontinent. I didn't like her, because I had known her before she fell ill and I'd thought she was haughty and unpleasant. Completely different from Brother Pouk.

Besides, I was sickened by the thought that she was five years older than Pol Pot. I'd never heard of a marriage in which the woman was older than the man. People used to say behind their backs that Auntie Ponnary must have cast a spell on Brother Pouk.

I don't believe in magic, but I too thought Brother Pouk could have chosen a better wife for himself, especially because she wasn't particularly good-looking. I don't mean to say that she was ugly, but you wouldn't want to look at her for long. Many of the girls who worked at our base were prettier, jollier, younger, and far more suitable as a wife.

But of course I never said that to anyone.

I may not have liked Auntie Ponnary, but for some reason she took a liking to me.

One day, when she was in one of her phases of going on about the Vietnamese, one of Brother Pouk's adjutants asked if I would please come and try to calm her down.

"How am I supposed to do that?" I responded angrily, because I had no desire to help.

"She likes you. Just go and sit with her," replied the adjutant.

So off I went, and she really did calm down a bit. She let me comb her hair and feed her. I stayed the night with her, and she didn't shout. So the next night I took my rattan mat to her hut and slept there, under a blanket.

This went on for several days, until one night I woke up and saw that Auntie Ponnary wasn't asleep but was looking at me.

She was sitting up on her mat, her eyes were open, and she was staring at me as if she thought I were a Vietnamese who'd come to kill her.

I was terrified. I didn't raise my head but went on lying there with my eyes wide open, watching to see what she would do.

I didn't sleep another wink all night. Nor did Auntie Ponnary. At sunrise I ran off to make breakfast—for her and for our leaders.

Living like that was utterly exhausting.

Luckily, six months later I came down with a high temperature and turned out to be suffering from malaria.

And a good thing too. I preferred malaria to Auntie Ponnary.

10.

It's hard to imagine a more unstable country than Cambodia in the 1960s and 1970s. Tons of American bombs were dropping from the sky, more and more of the country was shifting into the hands of the communist guerrillas, and on top of that General Lon Nol staged a lightning coup d'état and deposed Prince Sihanouk.

Sihanouk fled to China. The Chinese communists decided that in this situation his best move was to form an alliance with the Khmer Rouge, who had been his sworn enemies until then.

For Sihanouk, joining up with the communist guerrillas, who for years had been gathering in the jungle to overthrow him, was the only way to continue to have any significance in Cambodian politics. For the Khmer Rouge, a union with the hated prince had huge propaganda value: the Cambodian peasants believed the royal family brought and took away the rain, so they were afraid that after Lon Nol's coup the land would lose its fertility. Thanks to the alliance with Sihanouk, the number of Khmer Rouge support- ers began to rise even higher.

In 1971, the Khmer Rouge took Sihanouk on a tour of the terri- tory they had captured. It was a great experience for him and for the people who met him on the way. Including Auntie Moeun.

I accompanied him throughout that time as a cook. I was very pleased to meet him and to be able to get a close look at him.

The other cook on that trip was Yun Yat, wife of Son Sen, who was later the minister of defense, and we spent a long time discussing what we would make for the prince: some- thing traditional and Khmer, and at the same time something he would like.

Sihanouk turned out to be very nice, but he didn't want to eat our food. He had brought his own food with him from China—ready meals in cans, along with butter and sponge cake. One person from his entourage baked fresh rolls for him every day; in France those rolls are called baguettes. It looked to me as if our leaders, who were familiar with baguettes from their days as students in Paris, envied him those rolls. None of them said a word, but they kept glancing at them.

He never tried our dishes, not once; he ate only the canned food and the rolls. It was such a shame! Our prince refuses to eat the food offered him by the Cambodian peasants who have come out in crowds to greet him?

At the time I thought he was afraid of being poisoned.

It was only some years later, in China, when I had the chance to observe him on a daily basis, that I realized he simply despised our cuisine.

11.

People in sandals made of car tires captured city after city. The citizens received them joyfully. They believed the newcomers were bringing peace.

According to Peang Sophi, a citizen of Batdambang, there was a holiday atmosphere in the air. It was April 1975. Peang and his friends ran out to greet the guerrillas who had just taken their city. Peang didn't know much about them. He remembered that the young revolutionaries were afraid of cans. "Something in a tin [perhaps insecticide] had made one of them sick, so they mistook a can of sardines, with a picture of a fish on it, for fish poison, and one of them asked a friend of mine to throw it out. I saw them eating toothpaste once," he recalled.*

Other witnesses saw the guerrillas drinking the water out of toilet bowls.

On April 17 they captured Phnom Penh and immediately set about one of the standard projects of their revolution: resettling the citizens from the cities to the countryside, where they planned to create the new man. They rounded people up in the streets without warning, herded them into columns, and sent them off to the coun-

---

* Ben Kiernan and Chanthou Boua, eds., *Peasants and Politics in Kampuchea, 1942–1981* (M. E. Sharpe, 1982), 320.

tryside. They burst into other people's houses and gave them only a few minutes to gather the most essential things before taking them away. They said it was for their safety, because the Americans were planning to bomb Phnom Penh. They promised that in a few days they'd all be able to go home.

But they were lying.

At first, they did very little killing; only people from Lon Nol's regime were executed, and patients from the hospital who couldn't walk to the countryside unaided.

They also took away people's shoes and eyeglasses. For them, both of these items were relics of capitalism—an expression of the individualism that the new, better Cambodia was to escape. The piles of shoes torn from people's feet in those first few days of the new regime went on lying in the streets of Phnom Penh for many years.

Nuon Varin taught French at one of the private high schools in Phnom Penh. For years she had sympathized with the Khmer Rouge, so when the guerrillas took the capital, she and a group of her friends and students went out to greet them. Her account was recorded a few years later by the Polish reporter Wiesław Górnicki at a Vietnamese camp for refugees from Cambodia. "She was stopped by a Khmer Rouge patrol," he wrote, "and told to join a group of frightened, bewildered people. Neither her protests, nor her references to the children left at home were of any help . . . ; the soldier struck her on the back with his rifle butt, ordered her to take off her shoes, throw away her documents, and move off with the column."*

---

* Wiesław Górnicki, *Bambusowa klepsydra* [The bamboo hourglass] (Państwowy Instytut Wydawniczy, 1980), 112.

Nuon Varin tried arguing with the Khmer Rouge. As punishment she was assigned to Po Pet, one of the worst penal colonies. There she was constantly hungry. "She was given one hundred grams [3.5 ounces] of rice each day, once a month an egg, and sometimes, very irregularly, a bowl of *prahok*, a peasant soup made with soya noodles, vegetables, and pieces of fish. But there were whole weeks when the commune kitchen issued eighty grams [2.8 ounces] of rice per day . . . and nothing else."

12.

I had a serious case of malaria. Afterward, I had to walk around leaning on a stick for many months. The brothers said I came close to dying.

I only survived because Pol Pot gave me his pills. He didn't have many, but he shared them with me.

So I managed to escape death, but I couldn't hide from Auntie Ponnary. When I got better, Pol Pot didn't want her—and the Vietnamese who appeared in her head—to stop him from working. He appointed her president of the Women's Association. And I was made her secretary.

I thought I would cry with rage!

But Pol Pot could see that Auntie Ponnary liked to spend time with me. Angkar wanted me to work with her.

Angkar is me.

I am Angkar.

There was no arguing.

My main task was to keep her as far as possible from the leaders. I already knew she liked children. She and Pol Pot couldn't have their own; before their marriage Auntie Pon-nary had had cancer, and her ovaries had been removed.

It occurred to me that the presence of children might calm her down, so I organized some meetings for her in villages we had liberated. The children sang for her, recited poems, and then sat and told us what their lives were like. She sang with them. She loved to hear the children's stories.

During those outings of ours, Auntie Ponnary never talked about her Vietnamese. She never shouted or went unwashed. Yes, on some days it was difficult to communicate with her. She would seem absent; the children would sing for her, but she'd just stare at the wall, as if she weren't there. Some-times she'd suddenly ask me, "Where is Comrade Sâr? Is he safe?" Or, "Can you take me to him?"

But it was far better than the sleepless nights at the camp.

Later we'd go back to Pol Pot, and Auntie would tell him everything she'd heard in the village, every detail. In those brief moments I saw her just as she must have been when Comrade Pouk fell in love with her: quick-witted, intelligent, an excellent observer.

But after a week or more at the camp, she'd start seeing enemies everywhere again, so we'd have to go on the road again. And again.

Until one day, when I was in Kampong Cham province, one of the younger boys ran up to me, shouting, "Sister! Sister!"

"What is it?" I asked.

"Phnom Penh has been captured!" he cried, and then ran on.

Of course the first person I thought of was Pol Pot. I was pleased, because I knew it was a great day for him. But I was also worried about him. I knew how much he cared about people, how he couldn't sleep at night. I figured that now that he was going to take responsibility for the entire country, he'd have even more worries than ever. And that while he would be taking care of everyone else, he had no one at his side to take care of him.

13.

They pissed into a small pot. By the time it was full, the piss at the bottom would have started to ferment. Even Ieng Sary, minister of foreign affairs, pissed that way. "One can imagine the odor!" wrote Laurence Picq, who was the wife of one of the senior Khmer Rouge officials and the only person from the West to have personally experienced Pol Pot's regime, in Phnom Penh. First she was a cook, and then she was an interpreter. She also helped in the garden. The officials from the Ministry of Foreign Affairs pissed into that pot as a way of providing fertilizer for her plants.

The best way to demonstrate that you were a good communist was to clean the toilets—regarded in Khmer culture as one of the most offensive chores. The most daring cleaned them with their bare hands and scraped excrement off the walls with their nails. No wonder they did it: they were fighting for their lives.

Picq also recalls taking part in daily self-criticism sessions that lasted for several hours, with everyone confessing to more or less imaginary sins and informing on their friends.

At one of these sessions, a man suspected of stealing corn appeared. He confessed that once, when he was starving, he happened to have broken off a single cob and cooked and eaten it. He and his wife were sent to the countryside. "They had not returned," writes Picq. "People said they must have been traitors to have been so hungry!"*

In Cambodia under the Khmer Rouge, "they had not returned" meant death.

While the Khmer Rouge were in power, acute hunger prevailed—even at the Ministry of Foreign Affairs, known in the nomenclature of the time as B1. When new rice arrived, the employees shouted, "Long live Angkar! Long live the economic line! Long live collectivization!"

But often the rice did not arrive.

So a cook whose name was Sean made soups from herbs, banana tree trunks, and grass. But there were days when she had absolutely nothing to put in the pot. Or when they received nothing but one basket of rotten eggs and one of moldy fruit.

Picq made an important discovery: the Khmer Rouge used hunger as a political instrument.

Hunger was the penalty for disobedience.

Hunger was the penalty for bad origins.

Hunger was the penalty for sickness: for being unfit for the revolution.

Hunger helped them to maintain discipline.

"Hunger haunted all of our thoughts . . . Our bodies could not help but be grateful to Angkar. The Khmer Rouge had claimed their revolution would mean everyone had plenty to eat. But because of them, everyone went hungry"†

The menu at the ministry changed only when the political

---

* Laurence Picq, *Beyond the Horizon: Five Years with the Khmer Rouge*, trans. Patricia Norland (St. Martin's Press, 1989), 110.
† Ibid., 106.

seminars began. Then a special vehicle brought fish, vegetables, and even lobster.

In 1975, Yong Moeun and her husband, Pich Cheang, attended one of the first of these training sessions with a group of distinguished revolutionaries. They were known as the *bang*, or elders. The *bang* were housed not with the other B1 employees but in villas that had once been home to the local bourgeoisie. They weren't just better fed—on chicken, pork, and rice—but also given wine, and, according to Picq, their bodyguards went to fetch fresh white bread baked especially for them.

Meanwhile, the ordinary Cambodians were dying of starvation.

The topics of the seminars attended by Moeun and her husband included Angkar's visionary nature and farsightedness, the evacuation of the cities and its (exclusively positive) consequences, the abolition of money, and the role of Prince Sihanouk. Pol Pot personally explained to the *bang* that Sihanouk was a hostage of the Khmer Rouge and that he would be exploited by them as they wished; he was a tiger trapped in a cage.

"The Cambodian revolution has no historical precedent," said the Khmer Rouge.

"The permanent division of the cities and the countryside is final."

"Angkar is superior to Lenin and goes farther than Mao."

"The whole world is watching Angkar, because its revolution is the finest and purest."

14.

I was summoned to Phnom Penh two months after its capture. My husband was already there. First he was made head of the Central Bank, but later our executive decided that we would be the first country in the world where there was no money, and the Central Bank would cease to be necessary.

At that point we were both sent for training.

Before it began, I asked Pol Pot, "Why do I need these seminars? I want to cook!"

Brother Pol Pot smiled. "Angkar needs you for something else, Sister Moeun," he said. "Brother Pich Cheang is going to be our ambassador in China. You're going to be an ambassador's wife."

I didn't even know what an ambassador was.

So I said, "I don't want to go anywhere. I want to stay here, in Cambodia! I want to go on cooking for the leaders."

But Pol Pot just smiled.

"Sister Ly Kim Seng, Nuon Chea's wife, will cook for us now. I have a different task for you."

It was hard for me; I think I shed a few tears. But I wasn't going to argue like a fool. Angkar knew better what was good for us and what to demand of us. We'd go to China, and we'd see.

I knew I was doing it for the party. And for the revolution. And, like everything in my life, for Brother Pol Pot.

15.

The *éminence grise* at B1 was a woman named Roeun. Her husband, Doeun, was head of the Bureau of Commerce at the Ministry of Industry. It was he who had secured a job for his wife as head of a store for diplomats.* The status of the resourceful and enterprising Roeun rose by the week, until at some point she became the right hand of Ieng Sary, and thus responsible for the entire administration of B1. She brought in her cousins and other relatives and assigned them to an increasing number of positions.

Laurence Picq mentions that while working in the garden, she managed to grow several beds of very nice cabbages. Almost at once Roeun appeared, and instead of sharing the cabbages with the starving ministry employees, she took the whole lot away to her store for diplomats.

"Roeun was one of those people who float to the surface of every war or revolution," says the historian Soeum Borey. "Her only concern was how she could gain from it, and how much. Nobody controlled the money earned by the diplomats' store. And her cousins, who occupied more and more posts, began to form a peculiar clan that made sure her power grew."

Coincidentally, Moeun, Pol Pot's cook, was Roeun's niece, and the embassy in China was the most prestigious diplomatic post of all those to which the new Cambodian government sent its diplomats. Pich Cheang owed his appointment as ambassador exclusively to the fact that Roeun wanted to send her niece there.†

The nepotism that had so annoyed the Cambodian communists within Prince Sihanouk's circle had soon crept into their own ranks.

---

* For more on this topic, and on other situations where nepotism was rife among the leaders of the Khmer Rouge, see Serge Thion, "The Pattern of Cambodian Politics," in *The Cambodian Agony*, ed. David A. Ablin and Marlowe Hood (M. E. Sharpe, 1990), 149–64.

† Ibid.

16.

Three times I asked Moeun about Roeun, about their relationship, and whether it was thanks to Roeun that her husband had become an ambassador.

Three times, Moeun—in typical Khmer style—pretended not to have heard the question.

17.

Before leaving, we had a farewell meeting with the leaders. And there Brother Pol Pot surprised me by appointing me head of the Communist Party cell at the embassy. In other words, he'd made me Pich Cheang's superior. Everyone knew the party was the most important thing of all, and now my husband was lower down in the party than I was. He was the ambassador, but I was the one who'd preside at party cell meetings, while he'd have to sit and listen. When Pol Pot came to visit us in Beijing, he appointed me deputy ambassador and asked my husband with a laugh if he was obeying my instructions.

In Beijing, I worked very hard. After a year I began to speak Chinese, and after two years I was pretty good at it. I even translated some Chinese movies into Khmer. But that was nothing compared with my husband. He mastered Chinese in less than a year; he even amazed our Chinese comrades.

A year after we arrived in Beijing, our first son was born. We had two more sons after that. They all went to Chinese schools, and to this day they all speak excellent Chinese.

The only thing that made me feel awkward was not having to do anything for myself—neither the laundry, nor the ironing, nor the cooking. Everything was done by the staff employed by the Chinese.

But what I found strangest of all was that we had a cook. His name was Lao Song, and he was highly skilled. He cooked us nothing but Chinese food: beans, cabbage, chicken, and dumplings.

Lao Song was a much better cook than I was, so if I had time, I'd ask him to show me how to make some of the dishes. That's how I learned to make dumplings and spring rolls.

18.

In Phnom Penh I arrange to meet Prak and Keo, who are brothers and the friends of some friends of mine, and who miraculously survived the years of the Khmer Rouge regime. Prak works as a guide, taking tourists all over Cambodia—from the ancient temples at Angkor Wat, to Kratié province, where they watch the river dolphins, to the capital, Phnom Penh, and the coastal city of Sihanoukville.

Keo works as a bank manager, but his real passion is motorbikes. Until recently it was difficult to ride at a decent speed in Cambodia; the Khmer Rouge destroyed most of the roads, as a relic of imperialism, so Keo used to go to Thailand for his motorcycling adventures. He has had two serious accidents and both times made a miraculous recovery, but he'll never give it up.

"If you've grown up in captivity, for the rest of your life you can't get your fill of freedom," he says.

We're sitting in one of the best restaurants in the capital. We each order a bowl of sweet-and-sour soup and start to talk about the days when the Khmer Rouge were in power, when both brothers were children.

"In 1975, when Pol Pot came to power, I was eighteen months old," says Prak. "Mom was still breast-feeding me. When she realized they'd sent her to a commune where there were problems getting food, she was determined to make sure I had enough to eat."

"We know about this from a woman who was at the commune with our mother and whom we met by chance many years later," says Keo. "Prak doesn't remember, nor do I. The Khmer Rouge took great care to make sure that husbands and wives, brothers and sisters, and former neighbors didn't live in the same commune. They wanted to build a whole new society, so they broke all the old ties. And as a teenager I was sent to a completely different place from Prak and our mother."

"I did spend nights with my mother," says Prak. "I'm sure of that."

"But that wasn't inevitable either, because they often separated even small children from their parents, and the party, or some guardians working for it, raised them," says Keo. "Perhaps our mother was already sick if they allowed you to stay together at night? We don't know the details. By then I had been sent off to work with the adults. My job was to harvest rice, from daybreak to nightfall. We were in a good social category, the second, because our mother had managed to hide the fact that our father had been in the military."

"She gave the Khmer Rouge the name of a friend of hers who had died a few months earlier. Nobody realized," says Prak.

"Our father was killed during the civil war, fighting against the Khmer Rouge. If they'd found out the truth, we'd never have survived," says Keo. "The food was just a handful of rice anyway, with some sort of gunk. Every day it was the same, tasteless. And there was no meat. No way was it enough for a growing boy doing such hard labor. So my friend Khim and I used to go rat hunting. It was top secret; if anyone had seen us, we'd have been in big trouble. We used to steal long pieces of wire and matches from the commune. Today it seems funny—imagine stealing matches—but at the time it was a big deal. We had to watch the guards for a week, find a spot from where they couldn't see the door into the kitchen, and be certain where they were. Then I'd stand on watch while Khim sneaked into the kitchen. He'd be gone for five minutes, and they were the longest five minutes of my life.

"Once we had the wire and the matches, we'd go on nocturnal hunting expeditions. You had to creep up and then wait quietly for the rats to appear. Then a swift flick of the wrist, and if we were in luck, we got some meat. We'd light a small campfire—making sure nobody would notice the smoke—and afterward we'd go back to the camp without being seen.

"Until one day, during an evening self-criticism session, one of the commanders started an investigation into who was stealing matches from the kitchen. I thought my heart would leap out of my chest. Luckily, some other people from the camp began to accuse the cooks. Khim and I didn't say a word. The women who cooked for us got the blame. They bore some sort of punishment for it; I can't remember the details. I think one of them was transferred to another camp. How do I feel about it? Today I feel foolish, but you can't apply normal standards to such abnormal times. We were all fighting to survive.

"Later, Khim was killed anyway. I don't know what for. One day he simply vanished and never reappeared. Maybe they found the matches on him? I really don't know.

"You know, now I think that if they'd been smart, they'd have let people hunt rats. Those animals destroyed the crops and the grain, and the people were so hungry they'd have killed them all. For us, a roasted rat was a delicacy. I've eaten them several times at really expensive restaurants in various places, like Bangkok and Beijing. But in all my life nothing has ever tasted as good as the rats at the camp."

"I didn't know that, about the rats," says Prak.

"I told you. You've clearly forgotten."

"I didn't know . . ."

"Yes, you did. Every time we leave Phnom Penh to visit our aunt in Batdambang, there's a place by the road that sells rats, three for a dollar. And at that place I always tell you that story, and I say that one day we'll stop, so you can try roasted rat, little brother. Because until you've tried it, you know nothing about life. It's not so bad. You just have to overcome your disgust . . ."

"I never knew," insists Prak.

"You've just put it out of your mind," says his brother. "And a good thing too; it's better not to remember. I'd have forgotten about it if I only knew how."

"I don't remember the Khmer Rouge regime," says Prak. "I was too small. All I remember is when Mom died."

"She'd been sick for ages by then. We know that from the woman from the commune. Nobody could say what was wrong with her. The Khmer Rouge had killed all the doctors, and the only medical aid at the commune was provided by a boy of my age, who'd had a few days' training in how to give injections and how to lance boils. But our mother didn't have any boils; he couldn't have lanced anything for her. And there weren't any injections. Nobody was able to say what was wrong with her."

"One morning I awoke and cuddled up to her. I put my hand on her and waited for her to do the same.

"But she didn't cuddle me. I started sleepily searching for her breast. I don't think she was feeding me anymore, but I was still instinctively soothing myself at night by sucking her breast.

"But her breast was cold.

"I woke up and started shaking her. 'Momma!' I cried. 'Momma, wake up!'

"But she didn't.

"I couldn't understand what was wrong. I started crying.

"That was my first childhood memory. The first thing I remember. My mother's stiff hands."

"Oh, Prak, my brother . . . Because you're able to forget, which not everybody is, forget that. Why the hell should you remember that?"

19.

In the days of the Khmer Rouge, people didn't eat just rats.

They ate locusts, crickets, worms, red ants, and their eggs.

They caught tarantulas in the jungle and boiled them or roasted them on the fire.

They wrapped frogs in banana leaves, just as before 1975 they had wrapped fish or various kinds of meat, and baked them.

They ate elephants, turtles, lizards, water snakes and other snakes too, scorpions, and soup made of termite eggs.

They ate boiled or baked bats, and even drank their blood, believing—because bats eat a lot of fruit—it would give them strength and good health.

During the Khmer Rouge regime, people ate almost all the Ir-rawaddy River dolphins—the only, very rare freshwater and salt-water species. Of many thousands, there are just a few hundred left today.

They ate all sorts of birds, whatever they could catch, and also their eggs.

20.

Koy Thuon, Auntie Moeun's cousin who got her to join Angkar and was, as Moeun says, one of the nicest people she has ever known, was also the first victim of the purges among the high-ranking leaders. In 1977, he was arrested. He ended up at S-21, a prison that nobody ever left. Situated close to the center of Phnom Penh, it was set aside for the worst enemies of the regime, most of whom were former members of the Khmer Rouge who had been accused of treachery. Koy Thuon confessed to having planned to assassinate Pol Pot and to seeking support from the Thais, Americans, and Vietnamese.

"In these situations the entire family was punished—brothers, sisters, even people who came into accidental contact with the accused," says Soeum Borey. "When it came to the purges, everyone who had any connection with the traitor disappeared."

In Koy Thuon's case, his pregnant daughter was killed. And people whom he had encouraged to join the revolution in the guerrilla days. Their only sin was that they'd been brought into Angkar by the wrong person.

Among them were Roeun and her husband, Doeun. One day, both of them simply vanished.

A distant connection with one of the accused was enough for you to lose your life. Roeun's assistant's husband, Phât, took care of the rabbits that were raised in the yard at B1. He and his wife weren't killed along with Roeun, and he realized he would live as long as the rabbits were alive. So he cared for them to the very best of his ability.

One day the rabbits' eyes began to swell. The rabbits turned out to be infected with myxomatosis, an incurable virus. Phât had had nothing to do with it, but nevertheless he, his wife, and their baby disappeared.*

21.

When I found out Koy Thuon was dead, I was knocked off my feet.

Later the news reached me that the other ambassadors, our colleagues from the training course at B1, had been re-called to Phnom Penh with their wives. None of them came back from there. Yom and Din, who were at the embassy in Laos. Cheang and Touch, who were in Vietnam. Yaem and Ni, who'd been in North Korea. They were all executed.

It was said they'd been spying. For the Vietnamese, for the Americans, for the Russians. Was it true? Perhaps there was something to it. Or perhaps someone had made a mistake and condemned innocent people. At the time Cambodia had lots of enemies. The Americans had never come to terms with the fact that their bombing raids had achieved nothing. The So-viet Union and Vietnam were also unable to accept that we wanted to decide our own future. Can it be possible that everyone was a traitor except for us?

I don't know . . .

* Picq, *Beyond the Horizon*, 99.

At the time, I expected us to be next. I was sure that soon someone would come and hand us a letter, and we'd have to go back to Phnom Penh too.

And I'll tell you something.

I'd have boarded that plane.

My husband and I were very much liked by the Chinese, and several people made it clear to us that we could count on them. That they'd try to hide us, take us to another country perhaps, help us escape.

I always cut those conversations short. I would never have agreed to that.

Angkar is me. I am Angkar.

If Angkar had wanted me to go back, I'd have boarded that plane.

If Angkar had decided I should go to jail, I'd have gone to jail.

If Angkar had decided I had committed treason, I'd have agreed with Angkar.

As Ieng Sary said, Angkar has a hundred eyes, like a pineapple. Do I have a hundred eyes? No. So I believed that Angkar saw more and knew better.

And if Angkar had decided I must die, I'd have died.

I never talked to my husband about it, not even when he was no longer the ambassador, not even when Pol Pot was dead and we were living here, in Anlong Veng; we never revisited those days in our conversations. But I know he thought exactly as I did.

But no one summoned us. We never got a letter. We went on living.

22.

After Koy Thuon's death the Khmer Rouge were in power for only one more year.

Auntie Ponnary's nightmare came true: the Vietnamese really did appear. In a matter of days, they took Phnom Penh, which would supposedly never surrender, and Pol Pot's revolution ended like a bad dream. Step by step, the Vietnamese uncovered more and more of the crimes committed by their former comrades.

But although everyone knew what they had done, for a long time to come, the world continued to regard the Khmer Rouge as Cambodia's legitimate government. Pol Pot and the revolutionaries loyal to him returned to their jungle bases, from where they tried in vain to regain power and—successfully—traded in timber and precious stones, thanks to which they made a pretty good fortune.

Meanwhile, the West suspended the United Nations inquiry into their crimes, mainly to weaken communist Vietnam, with which the United States still had a bone to pick.

One of the architects of this policy was Zbigniew Brzezinski, at the time President Carter's national security adviser.

23.

The fall of Phnom Penh? A few days beforehand, we knew it was going to happen.

The Somali, Senegalese, and Sudanese ambassadors, who were our friends, came to see my husband and said, "You can see on the satellite pictures that Vietnam is gathering very large forces on the border."

My husband replied that even if it was true, the Vietnamese would be severely disappointed, because our army was well prepared for an attack.

Well, it wasn't.

When the Vietnamese marched into Phnom Penh, Sihanouk, whom Pol Pot was trying to save from being taken prisoner, appeared in Beijing. Pich Cheang went to fetch him from the airport. The Chinese provided a separate residence for the prince, but he was terribly bored there, so he used to come to the embassy. My husband learned to play tennis specially for him, because he was always dropping hints. The prince was like a great big child: look at me, aren't I amazing, aren't I clever, look how superbly I play! He grumbled about almost everything, but somehow he took a shine to me—I don't know why. And he'd say to me, "Madame, you're the only one who cares about me."

He'd smile as he said it, like a great big baby.

Whenever he lost at tennis he'd get mad, throw his racket to the ground, and refuse to speak to us for the next two weeks. But after that he'd be back, as if nothing had ever been wrong.

Pol Pot lost everything and fled into the jungle to escape the Vietnamese, while my husband played tennis with Sihanouk. It was all like something out of a bad dream.

Until one day a letter came from Ieng Sary, who was still the minister of foreign affairs, recalling my husband from the post of ambassador and summoning us back to Cambodia.

I knew what that sort of letter from Ieng Sary had meant a few years earlier. But by now it meant nothing more than what was written there: we were to go home.

24.

A jeep drove us to the next jungle base. At once we were taken to Pol Pot. He had aged, and he looked very tired. A lot of his hair had fallen out, and he was much weaker than the last time we'd seen each other in Beijing, but he was still a handsome man.

I didn't even ask if I should cook something for him. It was obvious. And when I put the food on the rattan mat, he looked at me, he looked at the plate, and he said, "Our Moeun hasn't cooked much at all. We're never going to get our fill." He was still joking around, just like in the days when we were twenty years younger. I was moved to tears. I could see that his dreams had not come true, the government was hunting him like a rat, he'd survived malaria again, and he was probably already suffering from the cancer that would be diagnosed a few months later. I knew the Vietnamese were spreading lies that he had killed people while he was in power. I can only guess how much he suffered when he heard that.

But I couldn't help him.

I was in tears, but I didn't want to make him sad. So I smiled at him. I smiled and wept all at once. And he looked at me and smiled, too, and went off to his house.

From then on, every time he saw me, he said, "What's happened to our Moeun? She always laughs at the sight of me." But now it was the other way around; every time I saw him I felt like crying.

I also noticed that Auntie Ponnary wasn't with him. They told me at the base that her condition had gotten much worse, so to avoid making Brother Pol Pot sad, she'd been taken to another part of the country.

A year later Pol Pot went away for twelve months to China, mainly to take care of his health. When he came back, he had stopped eating meat. The doctors there had advised him to give it up. For breakfast I made him fried noodles, oatmeal, and spring rolls; I had to get up at four to give them time to set.

For lunch he just had soup, usually a clear broth. Sometimes he had some fried or dried fish, but the only meat the Chinese doctors allowed him was black chicken; it's a species they have there, with black meat and blackish bones, and the Chinese believe that soup made from it gives you strength and good health. We got a few of those chickens from the Chinese, and our Khmer Loeu bred them for Pol Pot.

So I made him black chicken and melon broth. It's a very simple soup: you bone the chicken, and once the stock is simmering, you add sliced melon to it.

Soups were very important, because they soothed his stomach. But he only drank the clear broth; Nuon Chea or Ieng Sary had the meat.

It was bad. But the worst was yet to come.

25.

Mea Som was eighteen years old, with the round face of a village woman and muscles she developed while carrying artillery shells for the Khmer Rouge army. Someone noticed her in the dugouts and transferred her from among the soldiers to the leaders. Until

Auntie Moeun returned from her post in Beijing, it was Mea Som who cooked for Pol Pot and the other brothers.

Since their flight from Phnom Penh, Auntie Ponnary, Pol Pot's wife, had been living apart from him, in a place named Pailin. And because Mea Som was young and pretty, she caught Pol Pot's eye. The Angkar authorities made an exception for their leader and allowed him to divorce, agreeing that he should have a young wife to look after him in his old age.

Pol Pot became the next Khmer Rouge leader to marry a cook.

26.

It made me feel sad to set eyes on them. Very sad. Sister Som didn't look after him the way a wife should care for her husband. And she soon began to behave like the spoiled Sihanouk: she was the leader's wife, so she had a right to everything. Of course, she cooked for herself and for Pol Pot, but even so, everyone kept telling me, "Brother Pol Pot prefers your food. Don't be angry, Auntie. Make him something to eat."

But I was angry. I was cooking for a lot of people, and no one was in a hurry to help me. I wanted to ask them to transfer me from the leaders' camp to some other place. I was saying it out loud.

Ieng Sary heard me. And one day, he suddenly started talking to me about Koy Thuon.

"He betrayed us," he said. "Your cousin Koy Thuon wanted to sell us to the Americans."

I replied angrily that I wasn't in the country at the time and I had no idea what Koy Thuon had done.

Ieng Sary considered this for a while, and then he said, "I had a letter ready to be sent, summoning you back to the country. You and Comrade Pich Cheang."

That letter would have meant death. We both knew that.

"So why didn't you recall us?" I asked.

"Brother Pouk wouldn't let me," said Ieng Sary, smiling. "Eight times you were accused of treachery, Sister Moeun. Eight times various people said you'd betrayed us. Do you know why you were never recalled from Beijing?" he asked.

I didn't know.

"Because Brother Pol Pot said he wouldn't allow it. That if you were a traitor, then so was he. If we were going to arrest you, we should arrest him too."

It turned out Pol Pot had saved my life again. And I didn't even know.

Later I often wondered why Brother Sary told me that. Finally, I realized that it was because of Mea Som, Pol Pot's wife; Ieng Sary could see that I was hurt. And he wanted me to know that Pol Pot had been thinking about me. He wanted to console me.

From then on, I never wanted to leave Brother Mattress again.

27.

I saw Pol Pot's first wife, Auntie Ponnary, only once more, in Malai, in 1990. She knew who I was, which was strange, because we hadn't seen each other in more than fifteen years, and by then she didn't recognize anyone. Pol Pot had a child with his new wife, but Auntie Ponnary didn't know about that.

"Is Comrade Sâr all right? Is he safe?" she asked. "Can you take me to him? Take me to him. Please."

She didn't shout, just gazed at me imploringly. There were tears flowing from her eyes.

"Please," she repeated.

I didn't know how to answer. I left at the first opportunity.

28.

Pailin is the rapidly expanding capital for precious stones, over which towers a beautiful, richly adorned temple. The small town is surrounded by coffee plantations and taro fields.

Today, compared with the new buildings, the houses of the former revolutionary leaders, who came down from the mountains and promised they wouldn't fight against the government army anymore, look like the homes of poor relatives from a small village.

The first to turn traitor was Ieng Sary, Pol Pot's brother-in-law. It was August 1996 when Sary felt that the struggle no longer made sense, so he came to terms with Hun Sen, the new prime minister and former Khmer Rouge soldier installed by the Vietnamese. Sary was followed by Khieu Samphan and Nuon Chea.

To this day, in the surrounding jungle you might come upon large patches of chili peppers growing wild—a souvenir of the days when the Khmer Rouge soldiers, following their leaders' instructions, had done their best to leave edible plants behind them everywhere.

To this day, you might also come upon land mines. There are dozens of people living in Pailin who have lost a leg as a result of them. Although the Khmer Rouge capitulated twenty years ago, mines still explode around here.

Plenty of former Khmer Rouge soldiers live in Pailin, from the rank and file right up to the top brass. I invite two of them for lunch at a restaurant—former commanders of middle rank, Sum and Sang. I want to know what they ate in Pol Pot's day.

Sum is a small, skinny man of over fifty. In the guerrillas his unit supervised the people who were collecting precious stones for the needs of the Khmer Rouge; he watched to make sure they didn't sell them for their own gain. In time, Sum began to manage well enough to be put in charge of selling the gemstones abroad.

Sang is a little taller. In the army he commanded a unit that attacked Batdambang, the nearest large city, several times.

Both surrendered along with Ieng Sary.

"I never ate as well in my life as in those days," says Sum dreamily.

We're eating eel soup with carrots, a local kind of cabbage, and spices I can't identify.

"Take eel, for example. My men used to set traps for them. They'd take a two- or three-yard piece of bamboo, fit a lure inside it, and block the opening so the eel couldn't get out. I could have had eel every day if I'd wanted. Nowadays it's a rare delicacy for me. Thank you very much for the invitation."

"Others hunted wild pigs in the jungle," says Sang. "But nowadays in a restaurant a portion of wild pig costs fifty thousand riels [about twelve dollars]. Eel soup costs thirty thousand. Thank you very much for inviting me too. I can only allow myself food like this from time to time, when business is going well; I can't afford to eat like this every day."

"Once a year we all went to the border with Thailand, where we had training sessions with Pol Pot and the other leaders," says Sum. "And he used to say, 'In order to survive, each of you must be able to cook, hunt, and obtain food.' And indeed, each of us had a mess tin, a spoon, and a knife in his pack. The mess tins could be put on the fire; we all knew how to cook something quickly."

"That was the secret of Pol Pot's genius," says Sang. "He had a vision of how to energize Cambodia, how to make it into a strong state again. But, oh dear . . . It didn't work."

Sang and Sum belch noisily—that's customary here: apparently, Pol Pot and his comrades belched after their meals—then reach for the toothpicks and start to pick their nicotine-stained teeth.

29.

Though betrayed by his closest comrades, gentle, smiling Brother Mattress did not stop killing.

Almost dead on his feet by now, he went on to order the assassination of several foreigners who had accidentally crossed the border between Thailand and territory controlled by the Khmer Rouge. Later, he ordered the killing of Son Sen, one of his most loyal and devoted men, whom everyone regarded as his successor but whom Pol Pot suspected of negotiating with the government behind his back. Son Sen was killed along with his wife, the leaders' former cook, and their children. A total of thirteen people from his immediate family were killed.

By killing Son Sen, Pol Pot passed sentence on himself.

Even his most die-hard supporters realized that no one was safe.

Ta Mok, one of the last high-ranking leaders of the Khmer

Rouge who still hadn't gone over to the government side, had no
intention of waiting to be next. He immediately shot three people
from Pol Pot's close circle, and he also locked Saroeun, the man
who had killed Son Sen, in a metal tiger cage and had it dropped
from the top of a hill.

30.

Son Sen? I don't believe Pol Pot could have killed him. He was
from the oldest, most loyal guerrilla group. He meant more to
Pol Pot than all the others. I was with him when he heard
about his death. His face went white. He let the glass drop
from his hand. He loved him very much.

It was Ta Mok who killed Son Sen, and he did it that way
in order to cast the blame on Pol Pot. Pol Pot trusted people
too much. And Ta Mok must have been a Vietnamese spy.

Soon after the death of Son Sen and his family, a messen-
ger came to us from Ta Mok and said we were to show up in
the jungle. He said there was going to be a trial of "the traitor
Pol Pot." Those were the words he used—can you imagine? A
little whippersnapper who wasn't even born when Pol Pot
began the struggle against the enemies of Cambodia was now
calling him a traitor.

I didn't go to the meeting. Nor did my husband. Ta Mok
could have had us shot for that. Everyone was afraid of him.
One time he had a group of children arrested because they'd
climbed a tree and picked papayas on the way to school. He'd
called them traitors—because papaya trees are common

property, and it's up to the Organization to decide who may eat the fruit and who may not. Never mind that there were plenty of papaya trees growing there and lots of fruit lying on the ground, rotting.

Apparently, things like that were happening all over Cambodia while Pol Pot was in power. I don't know, I wasn't in the country at the time, but if anything like that did happen, it certainly wasn't with his knowledge. Brother Pouk would never have allowed children to be arrested for wanting to eat papayas. Never. I knew Brother Pol Pot better than my own mother and father.

Pol Pot was not a murderer.

Pol Pot was a man with a dream.

He dreamed of a just world. A world where no one went hungry. A world where no one put on airs or thought himself better than others.

Pol Pot would never have taken people's food away. If anyone gave orders of that kind, it certainly wasn't him.

So although I knew that Ta Mok would be furious, I also knew what that meeting would be like. I knew that other little pip-squeaks like the one who'd been to our house would be there, discussing who was a traitor and who was not. I knew I would weep.

I refused to attend.

Although I could have ended up in a tiger cage myself, I stood by gentle Brother Pouk to the end, the man known to the world as Pol Pot.

And I stand by him to this day.

31.

The American journalist Nate Thayer is the only Western reporter to have succeeded in talking to Pol Pot, shortly before his death. Ta Mok treated the former leader like a bargaining chip; he was ready to hand him over to the government, as long as he could negotiate better conditions for the surrender. The fact that he gave a Western journalist access to the former leader was meant to demonstrate his goodwill.

Thayer went to see Pol Pot in his bamboo hut in the jungle. Many years later I asked Thayer about the encounter, and whether he remembered anything about the food during his visit.

"Pol Pot had a small vegetable garden tended by his wife and young daughter, and lived off smuggled Thai food. He drank Chinese tea with Thai salt. Their [the Khmer Rouge's] dirty little secret was that they loved Thai, Chinese, and Vietnamese food more than Khmer. They put on their 'best banquet' for me. It was imported Pringles in a can, water buffalo made into hamburgers, warm Sprite and Coca-Cola, and fake Johnnie Walker Black Label whiskey."

In his conversation with Thayer, Pol Pot did not confess to any of his crimes.

32.

Nowadays I mainly rest. I have cable television, and I like to watch soccer and wrestling. I like the English league— Chelsea, Arsenal . . . Then I feel happy. Maybe because I'm looking at strong, healthy young men? I've spent my whole life with men like that; in the guerrillas they were extremely muscular. When I look at today's young boys, I long for the men of the past. These days they look like chickens at the supermarket. No muscles.

If I were younger, I'd buy a ticket and fly to England to see Chelsea or Arsenal live. But that's not going to happen. The television will have to be enough.

So I like soccer, and I like American wrestling. I like it when John Cena fights. There's a soccer player I like who has the same gentle smile as Pol Pot. What's his name? I can't remember. Show me the famous soccer players and I'll tell you. Oh, it's this one! Messi . . . You can see for yourself that he smiles in exactly the same way.

I have everything I need. When we first came here to Anlong Veng from the mountains, my husband and I had nothing. We bought a piece of land, and with our own hands we cleared the trees and leveled the ground. Then, although neither of us had ever done farm work, we sowed and harvested rice together. We had one water buffalo, and then we bought two more.

Our house is right by the road, so to earn some extra cash, I used to buy gas, pour it into old plastic bottles, and sell it.

Now, thanks to our work, my children have a proper gas station.

There are also days when I don't turn on the TV, but just sit and reminisce. I remember the life I once had, the people I met, and the people whose hands I shook. I think about my husband, too, and my friends from the guerrilla days.

I also think about Pol Pot.

You ask if things might have worked out differently between us. I don't understand that question. It all worked out for the very best. For many years I could look at him every day; I could see him laughing and hear him joking. I could cook for him. And that really is a great deal.

You ask if I loved him.

After everything you've heard from me, you can give your own answer: How could anyone fail to love him?

33.

Nowadays the grave of the dictator who abolished money stands in the shadow of a huge, multistory casino. Soeum, my guide, recalls that several years ago someone offered to sell him one of Pol Pot's bones.

"It was a piece of his hand, apparently original, and the guy wanted a hundred dollars for it. The remains of Pol Pot's semi-cremated bones were lying about on the grave for years. Nobody was remotely interested in them, not even the local dogs. I only stopped seeing any a while ago."

I've been there twice. It looks dreadful, as if they still wanted to humiliate him after death.

His second wife, Mea Som, has only been there once, early in 2000. First she came to see me and asked, "Moeun, shall we cook something together for Brother Pol Pot?"

I smiled and said, "Of course."

Together we made him his favorite lunch: sweet-and-sour soup with pineapple and chili, and roast chicken.

I asked Mea Som if he could have taken his own life. That's what people were saying. Some people. Apparently, he knew Ta Mok was planning to kill him, so he took a very large dose of the medicine he had at his base to make sure he wouldn't wake up again. But Mea Som said it wasn't true. He'd had a heart attack.

We took it all to the place where he was cremated, because people in Cambodia believe that after death a person's soul needs feeding in order to move on to its next incarnation. I don't believe that. But many people do, so you have to act accordingly. His soul definitely isn't there anymore. As the monks say, after all these years it has gone into someone else. So maybe Pol Pot is alive somewhere in the world? He must be a teenager, or about twenty perhaps. I don't know where he is, but I'm sure we'll hear of him again.

Seasonings

Working on a book of this kind presents a number of difficulties, one of which is finding reliable sources of information. Of course, some published biographies of each of the dictators do exist, but I wouldn't call them exhaustive. Thanks to the work of Philip Short and David P. Chandler, we know a relatively large amount about Pol Pot and his regime. Fidel Castro is also the subject of some major publications by authors including Tad Szulc. Unfortunately, not very much has been written about Saddam Hussein yet. It's even harder to find reliable sources on the life of Idi Amin, in whose case it's sometimes impossible to tell the myths—many of them created by the subject himself—from the truth. But I had the hardest time finding information about Enver Hoxha, because Blendi Fevziu's book about him only skims the surface of his extraordinary life story.

Meanwhile, there's almost no writing at all about the actual chefs, other than a few publications that include *Teufelsköche: An den heißesten Herden der Welt* [The devil's cooks: working at the world's hottest ovens] by Juan Moreno, *Dictators' Dinners: A Bad Taste Guide to Entertaining Tyrants* by Victoria Clark, and some press articles.

An additional problem was that in their conversations with me the chefs sometimes contradicted the stories I knew from these sources, or told them a different way. That's what happened with Otonde Odera, whom Juan Moreno interviewed more than a decade before I did. An account of their meeting was published in the German weekly newsmagazine *Der Spiegel* and in Moreno's book. Several details of Moreno's version of Odera's life story differ from the version Odera gave me and that I have recorded here.

It was similar with Yong Moeun, who avoided answering some of my questions by simply ignoring them. The Cambodian journalist Thet Sambath interviewed her in 2001 about her acquaintance with Pol Pot's wife Khieu Ponnary ("The Story of Khieu Ponnary, Revolutionary and First Wife of Pol Pot," *The Cambodia Daily*, October 20, 2001). That account is not the same as the version I heard when I talked to her in 2017. Both also differ from what Laurence Picq writes about Moeun and her family. Because the divergences concern her family, I'm not going to give details, but I recommend Picq's book to anyone who is interested.

These differences aren't significant, and can probably be attributed to my interviewees' ages, but nevertheless there were enough of them that I had to adopt a strategy for dealing with them. I decided that a person has a right to tell their own life story the way they remember it (or want to remember it) years later. Of course, if I spotted inconsistencies, I asked about them. But if the interviewee decided that the truth was what they were telling me at that particular moment, I accepted it as such.

I used various methods to check my information. I read the

published sources, of course. Beyond that, I asked people who had met the dictators, or who knew how their regimes operated, to read my manuscript. Finally, I consulted experts who specialize in the history of the countries featured in the book. Their names are included in the acknowledgments.

I have made every effort to verify the events and scenes described in this book. Nonetheless, many of them (for example, the cooks' conversations with the dictators) cannot be confirmed by anyone. We simply have to trust the cooks, just as we would trust them if we met them and they cooked for us. We must allow them to tell their stories—and to remember them just as they wish to be remembered.

Iraq

Saïd K. Aburish, *Saddam Hussein: The Politics of Revenge* (Bloomsbury, 2001).

Roman Chałaczkiewicz, *Zmierzch dyktatora: Irak w moich oczach* [Twilight of a dictator: Iraq through my eyes] (Wydawnictwo Znak, 2008).

Efraim Karsh and Inari Rautsi, *Saddam Hussein: A Political Biography* (Grove Press, 2002).

Uganda

J. H. Driberg, *The Lango: A Nilotic Tribe of Uganda* (T. Fisher Unwin, 1923).

Iain Grahame, *Amin and Uganda: A Personal Memoir* (HarperCollins, 1980).

Kenneth Ingham, *Obote: A Political Biography* (Routledge, 1994).

Henry Kyemba, *A State of Blood: The Inside Story of Idi Amin's Reign of Fear* (Ace Books, 1977).

George Ivan Smith, *Ghosts of Kampala: The Rise and Fall of Idi Amin* (St. Martin's Press, 1980).

Albania

Tadeusz Czekalski, *Albania* (Trio, 2003).

Blendi Fevziu, *Enver Hoxha: The Iron Fist of Albania*, trans. Majlinda Nishku (I. B. Tauris, 2016).

Misha Glenny, *The Balkans: Nationalism, War, and the Great Powers, 1804–2012* (Granta, 2012).

Enver Hoxha, *The Khrushchevites: Memoirs* ("8 Nentori," 1980).

Ismail Kadare, *Chronicle in Stone*, trans. Arshi Pipa (Canongate, 2011).

Owen Pearson, *Albania as Dictatorship and Democracy: From Isolation to the Kosovo War*, vol. 3 of *Albania in the Twentieth Century: A History* (I. B. Tauris, 2007).

Arshi Pipa, *Albanian Stalinism: Ideo-political Aspects* (East European Monographs, 1990).

Cuba

Frei Betto, *Fidel and Religion: Conversations with Frei Betto on Marxism and Liberation Theology*, trans. Mary Todd (Ocean Press, 2006).

Anya von Bremzen, *Paladares: Recipes Inspired by the Private Restaurants of Cuba* (Harry N. Abrams, 2017).

Philip Brenner and Marguerite Rose Jiménez, eds., *A Contemporary Cuba Reader: Reinventing the Revolution* (Rowman & Littlefield, 2007).

Suzanne Cope, "When Revolution Came to the Kitchens of Cuba," *The Atlantic*, August 11, 2016, www.theatlantic.com/international/archive /2016/08/cuba-castro-villapol-julia-child/494342.

Servando Gonzalez, *The Secret Fidel Castro: Deconstructing the Symbol* (InteliBooks, 2016).

Che Guevara, *Che: The Diaries of Ernesto Che Guevara*, trans. Alexandra Keeble (Ocean Press, 2008).

Tom Miller, *Trading with the Enemy: A Yankee Travels Through Castro's Cuba* (Basic Books, 2008).

Juan Reinaldo Sanchez, *The Double Life of Fidel Castro: My 17 Years as Personal Bodyguard to El Líder Máximo*, with Axel Gyldén (St. Martin's Press, 2015).

Tad Szulc, *Fidel: A Critical Portrait* (Perennial, 2002).

Marisa Wilson, *Everyday Moral Economies: Food, Politics, and Scale in Cuba* (Wiley-Blackwell, 2013).

Cambodia

David A. Ablin and Marlowe Hood, eds., *The Cambodian Agony* (M. E. Sharpe, 1990).

William Burr and Jeffrey P. Kimball, *Nixon's Nuclear Specter: The Secret Alert of 1969, Madman Diplomacy, and the Vietnam War* (University Press of Kansas, 2015).

David P. Chandler, *Voices from S-21: Terror and History in Pol Pot's Secret Prison* (University of California Press, 2000).

Gina Chon and Sambath Thet, *Behind the Killing Fields: A Khmer Rouge Leader and One of His Victims* (University of Pennsylvania Press, 2010).

Wiesław Górnicki, *Bambusowa klepsydra* [The bamboo hourglass] (Państwowy Instytut Wydawniczy, 1980).

Ben Kiernan and Chanthou Boua, eds., *Peasants and Politics in Kampuchea, 1942–1981* (M. E. Sharpe, 1982).

Laurence Picq, *Beyond the Horizon: Five Years with the Khmer Rouge*, trans. Patricia Norland (St. Martin's Press, 1989).

Philip Short, *Pol Pot: The History of a Nightmare* (John Murray, 2006).

After-Dinner Mints

This book took four years to write, on four continents, and it would never have seen the light of day without the help of a large number of people.

In the first place I'd like to thank the dictators' chefs who agreed to talk to me.

I'd also like to thank my guides and interpreters who helped me on the ground. I chose them very carefully, because they not only had to find the cooks for me, which was no easy task, but also had to persuade them to talk to me. Thanks to them, I was able to visit each cook as if I were going to see an old friend. And thanks to their openness and competence, the cooks told us lots of things they had never told anyone before.

They are:

Iraq

Hassan Ashwor
Ibrahim Elias
Marcus Freeman

Uganda

Carl Odera

Julia Prus

Albania

Lindita Çela

Besar Likmeta

Cuba

Jorge Cotilla

Miguel X.

Cambodia

Yin Soeum

Thank you, too, to everyone who helped me while I was working on the book. I'm especially grateful to Katarzyna Boni, Soeum Borey, Ian Buruma, Sean Bye, Olga Chrebor, Ali Dib, Artur Domosławski, Paweł Goźliński, Major Iain Grahame, Tomasz Gudzowaty, Dorota Horodyska, Erjon Hysaj, Wojciech Jagielski, Hanna Jankowska, Zbyszek Jankowski, Izabella Kaluta, Marcin Kącki, Piotr Kędzierski, Ton van den Langkruis, Daniel Lis, Maciej Musiał, Paweł Pieniążek, Agnieszka Rasińska-Bóbr, Philip Short, Damian Strączek, Mariusz Szczygieł, Mariusz Tkaczyk, Renata Trzcińska, Mirek Wlekły, Ewa Wojciechowska, Małgosia Woźniak-Diederen, Hassan Yasin, Lucie Zakopalová, and Natalia Żaba.

Thank you to Penguin Random House, first and foremost my wonderful commissioning editor, John Siciliano, who believed in this book and bought the rights before I had started to write it, and also to my excellent line editor, Gretchen Schmid.

Thank you to my translator, Antonia Lloyd-Jones, who has done and continues to do a lot for me personally and for Polish literature. Thank you for your friendship and for the dedication with which you have translated this book. And for a very special day in East Anglia.

Thank you to Anna Dziewit-Meller and Marcin Meller for keeping me company on my literary journey almost from the start. Thank you, Marcin, for publishing the Polish edition of this book at Wydawnictwo W.A.B., where I've had the pleasure of working with a great team including Elżbieta Kalinowska, Dominika Cieśla-Szymańska, and Anna Dworak.

Thank you to my impresario, Gabrysia Niedzielska.

Thank you to my agents, Anna Rucińska and Marcin Biegaj, and the whole fabulous team at Andrew Nurnberg Associates. And also to Magda Dębowska, for whose agency I first started working on this book.

Izabela Meyza—thank you for being there. And I promise I really will learn to cook (or at least I'll try). I did learn a lot at Marcus's restaurant, but I've never learned to do it properly.

Thank you to Anielka, Marianka, Mama, Tata, Babcia, and Dziadek.

Writing this book has been a difficult but extraordinary journey, and I'm extremely grateful to everyone who has supported me along the way.

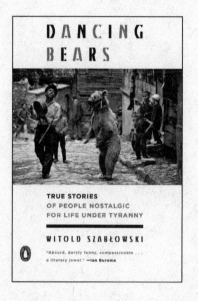